FINDING JOHN

ANDREW SERRA

Tudor City Press
New York

Cover Photo: Archive Image/Alamy Stock Photo
Cover Design by Annette Fiore DeFex

ISBN: 978-1-7322380-0-8
ISBN: 978-1-7322380-1-5 (ebook)

Library of Congress Control Number: 2018904631

Tudor City Press
New York, NY

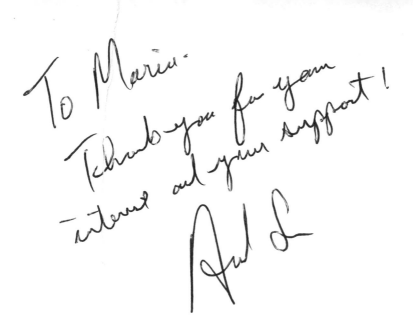

To Maria —
Thank you for your
interest and your support!

FINDING JOHN

*To all those whose hearts
were broken that Tuesday morning.*

CHAPTER 1

THE RAIN WAS STUBBORN. I had worked through the night and saw the dark sky lighten while March winds pushed the clouds away and the temperature rose. Still the rain fell—not in a downpour, but a mist. The thick dust that coated the pile and our clothes and eventually our lungs was wet on top but not all the way through. Once the damp outer layer was turned over, the macabre powder billowed up and filled our nostrils with a smell that has never left me. It lays dormant and unnoticed until I pass a construction site and catch a whiff similar to but not quite equal to the pulverized concrete and burnt flesh medley. I stood at attention for some time and my helmet was digging into my forehead but I didn't want to move to adjust it. I stared ahead and ignored the discomfort. On the ground lay a Stokes stretcher draped with an American flag. The stretcher would not be moved until the father of the firefighter whose remains it contained arrived.

We were called to attention because the new fire commissioner was arriving. His car drove down the ramp and straight up to within a few feet of the stretcher. Heavy equipment was moved up and down the ramp all the time but in my many months at the site, I had never seen a sedan use it. A rear door opened and an aide held an umbrella open as the commissioner stepped out and took hold of the handle. My gaze was drawn to his shoes—shiny leather dress shoes which left smooth footprints in the moist gravel clearing. Words I could not hear were exchanged with the battalion chief in charge of the recovery detail, while the firefighters and Port Authority cops who worked the overnight congregated nearby. Those shoes did not belong there. My boots were wet inside. They were caked with dust and cracked— they belonged. The firemen, cops, and ironworkers on the detail belonged. We didn't need to be driven up close to the stretcher to understand what we were doing there. But the World Trade Center rescue and recovery was never just about the victims or the responders. Politics were an omnipresent force and a bureaucrat's fancy shoes were the perfect metaphor for the converging forces that descended on those hallowed grounds.

The night had progressed like most others I had spent at the recovery detail. Cops and firemen would stand around a circle while an excavator pulled back debris from the twisted steely mess of "the pile." The excavator would unpeel small bites at a time so as not to further destroy any human remains found. The responders would then climb onto the small debris field the excavator had unearthed and pick through it. If remains were found, they were usually small pieces of bone or skin. The discovery of any remains was then followed by extra scrutiny of the area involved.

We worked through the night with little success. Most of what the excavator revealed was just twisted beams, dust, smashed office artifacts, and small slabs of rock. Clothing usually got our attention as a clue that remains were near, but on that night I don't remember finding much of anything beside a slight chill in the damp cool air. Then, just after dawn, everything changed.

I had just walked away from one excavator when out of the corner of my eye I noticed another excavator, thirty feet away or so, pull back a scoop of debris. The sleeve of a coat was caught by the bucket and stretched up before breaking free and snapping back to the ground. Around the sleeve was a reflective yellow and gray stripe— unmistakable to me. It was the sleeve of a firefighter's bunker coat. Another firefighter from my company, Rob Maddalone, and I ran over to the excavator and waved our arms furiously to get the operator's attention. He knew immediately what we wanted and he gingerly dumped the contents of his bucket next to the area he had just dug and swung the boom of his machine out of our way. Rob and I dug by hand. I held the coat's sleeve and clawed debris from around and underneath. It took a few minutes—the force with which the pile had been compressed down during the collapse made everything difficult to free by hand—but we were able to free the coat in one piece.

The Fire Department had begun printing firefighters' names on the back of their bunker coats just that summer. All new coats came with names but most firefighters at that point still had no name on their coat. The only way to know whose coat it was to open the front breast flap and read the magic marker imprint that the quartermaster used to write inside. I turned the flap open and saw the black, block letters. *Tipping.*

I sat back on a slab of rock, still holding the coat open, and stared at the name. *Who is Tipping?* I thought. I needed to know something about him. I opened one of the coat pockets and found a length of rope and a folding knife. I kept the same things in my bunker coat pocket. *Who is Tipping?* I put the knife and rope back in the pocket and set the coat down. Rob and I continued to dig—by hand. We were joined by Firefighter Bobby West, also from my company—Squad 1, and Lieutenant Steve Jezycki. I knew Steve because I had worked with his brother Mike in Ladder 131. His sister Peggy had been killed in the attacks and Steve and Mike spent a lot of time at the site trying to find her. Eventually we uncovered the bunker pants that belonged with the coat. The pants, however, were not empty. As I turned them over I soon discovered what had made the pants feel so heavy. It took a moment to process, but I realized that there on the pile, as the first hints of rain came down and the sun awakened in the east, I was holding something both gruesome and sacred. On my knees with trembling hands I beheld a dead firefighter.

Over our handie-talkies, we transmitted the location of our discovery. The notification process was undertaken by the officers staffing the office trailer serving as a command post. We placed the remains in a Stokes stretcher and draped a flag over the top and then waited. Somebody said he worked at Engine 54 and Ladder 4, in Midtown. The system in place then was that if the remains of a cop or firefighter could be identified, their command was notified and would respond immediately to carry the stretcher out of the pit. We knew 54 and 4 were on their way and we waited. No one touched the stretcher. It was for his brothers to carry him out. It was around this time I learned that Firefighter Tipping's father was a retired fireman and that he was also on his way.

The members of Engine 54 and Ladder 4 arrived and all work on the pile was called to a halt. Members of the FDNY, NYPD, and PAPD, as well as the construction workers made their way toward the ramp to line up. They would salute the fallen firefighter being carried out. With the men of 54 and 4 was Tipping's father. I cannot imagine his grief, but as I write these words many years after the fact, the memory I am struck with is the determination on his face. It must have taken all of his strength but he was determined to bring his son home. Next to the father was a uniformed police officer.

Somebody said that it was Tipping's brother, though it was in fact his brother-in-law. The important thing remained—Firefighter Tipping would be carried out by his family, both his firehouse family and his actual one.

I would later learn that the man we found that morning was named John J. Tipping II. I saw the grieving group gather around the stretcher and felt some small satisfaction that he was going back to his family. So many would never be found. It was an upside down world in which finding a body was a *good* day. It justified all of our work. Whether it was the remains of a fireman, or cop, or stockbroker, or dishwasher; recovery worked stopped and we solemnly marked the moment we knew at least one more family might find some degree of closure. Looking down at that flag-draped stretcher, I thought what everyone was probably thinking: *There goes a hero.*

From the cops and firefighters, to the tradesmen, to John Tipping's family and the members of 54 and 4 and even the new fire commissioner, nobody there that day could have imagined what lay in store for John Tipping in the months ahead. On the day he was found and at his funeral after, he was heralded as a selfless hero. In less than a year, however, he would be publicly shamed. John Tipping and the men of Ladder 4 would be shown to the world as the worst of villains. His Eighth Avenue firehouse—with its overflowing memorial of candles and flowers out front—had been a focal point for the world's sympathy. It would become the epicenter of a media firestorm.

Chapter 2

Just off Times Square, in the heart of the Theatre District at the corner of West 48th Street and Eighth Avenue sits the quarters of Engine 54, Ladder 4, and Battalion 9. The firefighters who work in this Seventies-era, two-story station claim the unofficial title of the busiest firehouse in the world—and they may very well be. First established in 1865, by 2001 Ladder 4 was responding to over four thousand fires and emergencies per year. The members of 54 and 4 are conditioned not only to constant running, but gridlocked traffic, immense crowds of New Year's revelers, and constant tourists' inquiries and photo taking. Their district is a complex amalgam of glass and steel high-rises, hundred-year old tenements, and theatres both old and new. It is not an easy place to work and the firefighters assigned there take pride in that fact. On September 11 all on-duty members of Engine 54, Ladder 4, and Battalion 9 were killed—15 men in total.

Lieutenant Daniel O'Callaghan was a 17-year veteran of the FDNY. It seems the only thing he was more devoted to than his job, were his wife Rhonda, and two children—a 6-year-old girl and 1-year-old boy. He loved to leave Post-It notes around the house for them to find while he was at work.[1] "He'd draw smiley faces on them,"[2] recalled Rhonda in an interview following the attacks, "and he'd write 'I love you' or 'I miss you' on them."[3] O'Callaghan was 42 years old.

Joseph Angelini Jr. was 38 and the son of Firefighter Joseph Angelini Sr., of Rescue 1 who was also killed in the attacks. He lived in Lindenhurst with his wife, Donna, and three young children—two girls and a boy. He was passionate about carpentry, gardening, and cooking. At the time of his death he was working on a dollhouse for one of his daughters.[4] "He was the air in my lungs, and now that air is taken away from me,"[5] Donna told a reporter. "I keep waiting for him to come off a 24 [hour shift] and come through the door and say, 'You wouldn't believe what happened to me today.'"[6]

Michael Lynch was 33 years old and lived in New Hyde Park, New York, with his wife, Denise, and two young sons—one was 3, the other less than a year old.[7] He was trusted by his officers as a dependable firefighter who was always on the straight and narrow path. But he was also trusted among his fellow firefighters because of his down-to-earth nature.[8] "He was someone an officer could tell to *do this* and then forget about it—and know it would be done the right way," his friend Tim Brown, who had worked with Lynch in Ladder 4, recalled. "Mike's bosses knew... He was just a friggin' great fireman."[9]

Michael Haub was 34 years old on September 11, 2001. He lived on Long Island with his wife, Erika, a 4-year-old son, and a 1-year-old daughter. Michael stood out among the other men in the firehouse for being fluent in German[10] and he enjoyed cooking German dishes in the firehouse.[11] Though he had only joined the FDNY two years before, Michael had served as a deputy chief with the Roslyn Heights Highlands Volunteer Fire Department.[12]

Samuel Oitice was 45. He lived in Peekskill, New York, with his wife, Jean, and two children. He joined the FDNY in 1983 after having been a police officer in Peekskill for four years. A sports enthusiast, he helped found a travel roller hockey league and still found time to volunteer for the Peekskill Fire Department.[13] Oitice had transferred in to Ladder 4 after spending a decade in the South Bronx and was so respected among the officers and members of 4 Truck that he quickly assumed the role of a senior man in the company despite being relatively new.[14]

Michael Brennan was 27 years old and grew up in Queens. A six-year veteran of the department, he was passionate about water sports and snowboarding. Coming from a large Irish family, Brennan reveled in swapping practical jokes with his brother.[15] Michael harbored a lifelong fascination with cops and firemen—his favorite TV show as a child was *CHiPs*.[16] When the Fire Department called in 1995, his dream came true.

John Tipping worked the night tour, Monday September 10. On an emergency call during the night, John had scratched his cornea and been placed on medical leave. Because it was late, he decided to sleep at the firehouse and catch a train the next morning.[17] He was about to leave the firehouse when he heard about the attacks.[18] When Ladder 4 was dispatched downtown, he jumped on the rig. He was 33 years old. These seven men rode Ladder 4's rig to the World Trade Center on September 11, 2001.*

**

Few events in our nation's history have received the amount of news coverage that the 9/11 attacks received. By 2001, the Internet and cable news' 24-hour programming were in full swing. The public had an unquenchable thirst for news stemming from the attacks and the media outlets churned out stories as fast as they

---

*Captain David Wooley, a 30-year veteran of the FDNY and longtime commander of Ladder 4 had traded shifts with a colleague and worked in Engine 54 on 9/11/01. He was killed as well.

could produce them. In just about every neighborhood in the city there was a firehouse with a makeshift memorial of candles and flowers out front. Some firehouses lost 15 or more members—the public's outpouring of sympathy was tremendous. These firehouses made for easy news stories in the days following the attacks. Any reporter or news crew could walk up to a firehouse and get a quick piece about a blue-collar guy, with a wife and kids at home, cut down in the prime of his life.

Three hundred and forty-three members of the FDNY died on 9/11—a staggering, unprecedented loss for a uniformed agency. The men who died had done so heroically and the public's genuine sympathy was mixed with a much-needed touch of inspiration. It was inspirational to hear stories of heroics amidst so much sadness. The media coverage of firefighters was intense and would eventually reach a saturation point. There were, of course, many heroes on 9/11: EMS workers and police officers, office workers, security and maintenance personnel—all heroes. The news stories, however, were disproportionally focused on firefighters. It would be impossible to scientifically graph the total number of news stories about 9/11 to determine the exact number of reports featuring firefighters. But anecdotally, using nothing other than my own memory and gut feeling, I thought the coverage was disproportional. I've spoken with family members who lost loved ones in the attacks—non-firefighters. More than once, I've heard that, in their view, it was possible to turn on the TV and think the only people who died were firemen. This may be an extreme interpretation and of course there were plenty of stories about victims of 9/11 from all walks of life. The point is that the amount of news coverage directed toward the Fire Department was massive. With increased   coverage   comes   increased   scrutiny.

Newspapers and media outlets ran with the "heroic fireman" story as far as they could. The time would then come when some decided the story needed to be pushed further. It was time to knock firefighters off their pedestal.

**

In September of 2001, William Langewiesche was a national correspondent for *The Atlantic Monthly* with many books and articles to his credit. A licensed pilot and world traveler, Langewiesche spent years reporting from some of the globe's most remote places.[19] The attacks of 9/11 brought his attention back to New York. Whether it was a sense of adventure, or curiosity, or a particular self-confidence that he could do the story justice, he was determined to get as close to the epicenter as possible. His editor sent faxes to City Hall and to the city's Department of Design and Construction on the off chance a press pass could be had.[20] Luckily for Langewicsche, the commissioner of the DDC at the time was Kenneth Holden, who happened to be a fan of the author's work.[21] In the immediate aftermath of the attack, the previously obscure DDC found itself in a lead role at the World Trade Center site and Langewiesche was given an all-access pass. From the very beginning to the last day of the rescue and recovery effort, he was there. He was the only journalist given access to the highest levels of the operation's hierarchy,[22] access that was provided by Holden.

Over the course of the next year, Langewiesche published a series of articles in *The Atlantic Monthly* about his experiences (these articles would later be compiled in the book *American Ground: Unbuilding the World Trade Center* in October of 2002.) *American Ground* is an insightful play by play of the rescue and recovery effort largely from the chief engineers' and construction managers' points of view. Langewiesche's acerbic prose is both elegant and straightforward. Before most of the public at large had even heard of Langewiesche's report, however, newspapers began focusing on one particular passage, in which the author describes how a fire truck was pulled up from the debris by an excavator and had its roof torn off revealing "dozens of new pairs of jeans from the Gap, a Trade Center store."[23]

"It was hard to avoid the conclusion," Langewiesche adds, "that the looting had begun even before the first tower fell, and that while hundreds of doomed firemen had climbed through the wounded buildings, this particular crew had been engaged in something else entirely..."[24]

**

The reaction was loud and immediate. Over 100 firefighters and family members protested Langewiesche at a book-signing event at the South Street Seaport. The New York tabloids covered the drama extensively. 'Liar!' read one *New York Post* headline, in quotation marks of course.[25] In the end, the media coverage merely ensured that the story spread—and not everybody was outraged by the allegations. Over the prior year, firefighters had protested everything from the scaling back of rescuers from the recovery effort to projected rebuilding designs. Many viewed the firefighters' outrage over Langewiesche's claims as just another protest at best, or a guttural reaction to an accusation that hit a little too close to home at worst. And then there were the other two-thirds of the recovery triangle (police and construction), many of whom had butted heads with firefighters at the site and saw these accusations as long-awaited vindication.

Protestors might have been able to disrupt a book signing, but they couldn't stop William Langewiesche from being praised in literary circles. "Truth, unclouded by sentiment," is how Jeffrey Goldberg described *American Ground* in a glowing review for *The New York Times*.[26] Goldberg especially liked the way the book treats "members of New York City's now sacrosanct Fire Department, who succumbed to greed and selfishness and divisiveness."[27] *Publishers Weekly* predicted "the exposure in the *Atlantic* and widespread review coverage may help this elegantly written and unique September 11 book rise toward the top."[28]

CHAPTER 3

I HAD AN OLD CLOCK RADIO on my nightstand set to go off at 9—plenty of time to have a cup of coffee and drive over to the College of Staten Island for my morning classes. A couple of weeks into the new semester, I was juggling my school and work schedules as best I could. Scheduled to work that Tuesday morning, I had traded shifts with another member of my company to be able to attend class. The clock radio now cracked to life and half-asleep I heard the DJ say something about a plane crashing into the World Trade Center.

Oh shit! I thought. My company, Ladder 131, was located in Red Hook, Brooklyn, right near the entrance to the Brooklyn-Battery Tunnel. I lay in bed and ran down the most likely chain of events in my mind. *A small charter-type plane flew off course and struck one of the towers. Maybe the pilot had had a heart attack or something and lost control.* Serious high-rise building fires in lower Manhattan had a preplanned response matrix that included Brooklyn companies. Engine 279 (also stationed in my firehouse) and Ladder 131 would surely be there. *Shit, I'm missing it,* I thought.

This last thought may seem odd to anyone not a firefighter. Firefighters spend years training and honing their skills. We pride ourselves in being ready to respond to any emergency at a moment's notice and would greatly prefer to be integral in mitigating the hazard than watching from the sidelines. I went downstairs and turned on the TV. The unforgettable image filled the screen—the North Tower was aflame. While I was watching, a massive fireball blew out the back of the South Tower. *What the hell was that?* I wondered. *Did some kind of generator or utility equipment catch fire from the flames of the North Tower?* The announcer was flustered with the news that a second plane had crashed into the World Trade Center. They showed new footage from a different camera angle—the plane flew directly into the building. *This is no charter-plane accident.* I decided to go to my firehouse and then the phone rang.

"Andy."

"Yeah, Dad."

"Did you hear?"

"Yeah, I got the TV on."

"I'm looking right at it."

At that time, my father drove a bulldozer at the Staten Island Landfill. On a clear day, the top of the dump offered a perfect view of the Manhattan skyline.

"The top looks crooked. Do you think it could fall over?"

"I'm sure it's not crooked," I answered, in denial. "The rising heat is probably warping the image."

I hung up and started getting dressed. The phone rang again.

"Yo."

It was my brother, Rob. He had just finished his training at the Fire Academy the day before and was due to start a field training rotation at a firehouse in Queens the following day. That Tuesday, however, he had off and was driving to Brooklyn to tryout for the FDNY hockey team. I didn't have to ask if he'd heard the news—I knew him well enough. The tone of his *Yo* told me that he knew.

"What's up?" I asked.

"What should I do?"

"Did you hear from the Academy?" I asked. He was still assigned to the Academy, though detailed to the Queens firehouse.

"No, should I call there? I'm on Hylan Boulevard, should I just go to Rescue 5 or your firehouse?"

"I'd call the Academy; they may want you to report to a staging area. Where's your gear?"

"Home," he answered. He had not yet started his training detail, so his bunker gear (protective, fire-resistant coat/pants set) and helmet were not at the firehouse.

"Go get it and call the Academy."

"Where are you going?"

"I'm going to 131 to get my gear."

I've thought about that phone call with my brother a lot over the years. With massive rescue efforts occurring simultaneously in two high-rise fires, all five of the city's rescue companies were eventually dispatched to the World Trade Center. On Staten Island, many off-duty firefighters responded to the quarters of Rescue 5. Rescue companies' trucks are specially designed to carry technical rescue equipment and coincidentally have room in the back for extra personnel. Quite a few of the off-duty firemen who showed up at Rescue 5 that morning jumped on the rig and rode to their death. Had he gone straight there, I don't know if Rob would have arrived at Rescue 5 in time to catch a ride with them, but it's something I think about. After retrieving his gear, Rob reported to two different firehouses, was sent to a hospital to donate blood, and then to the Staten Island Ferry terminal to await transport, which ended up being a city bus, not a ferry boat. He arrived at the Trade Center later in the day, manned a hose line, and later searched for body parts. His assignment that day would spare his life, but he would not come through unscathed.

I found the slip of paper I had with my brother Joe's phone number on it. He was sharing an apartment in Hoboken at the time and his roommate answered the phone. "He's at work," he told me. *Shit.* He worked right near the Trade Center.

I came out of my house to see groups of neighbors on their front lawns commiserating. It was as if the shock of the news would not be real until it was shared with the world outside. I saw the man who lived next door, a retired fireman.

"You're heading in?" he asked.

I nodded but my attention was drawn to the woman who rented the apartment in his basement. She was crying.

"I work there," she muttered between sobs. "I called out sick today."

I sped down Hylan Boulevard pausing only briefly at red lights. I was behind a man on a motorcycle wearing a FDNY Rescue 2 sweatshirt. I kept pace with the weaving Harley and reached the Verrazano Bridge just as Triborough officers were preparing to close the crossing. The motorcyclist weaved around stopped cars and I did my best to squeak my little Saturn through the maze. The officers must have noticed the sweatshirt and waved the motorcycle by. I held up my FDNY parking placard and was allowed through as well. The motorcyclist and I raced across the bridge. The unusually open roadway gave him the space he needed to leave me in the dust. I continued ahead until I came up behind a jam of cars at the bend were the Gowanus Expressway heads toward the Battery Tunnel and the BQE. A police car was blocking off a lane, which the officers were keeping clear. I turned into the lane and was waved over by one of the cops. I held up the placard and rolled down the window.

"Tunnel's closed," he announced.

"I'm just trying to get to my firehouse in Red Hook," I answered.

"Good luck," he said kindly, waving me through. "Stay safe," he added and then yelled out for the other cops to let me through. I made it to the exit ramp.

I parked near the firehouse—both Engine 279 and Ladder 131's rigs were gone. There was a flurry of activity, however, as all of the off-duty members were making their way in. I saw Firefighter Mike Golding by the front door. His eyes were watery.

"One of the towers collapsed," he told me. He motioned to the department radio in the housewatch. "A chauffeur was giving a Mayday that he was trapped in the rig."

Everyone was quickly assembling gear and stepping into their bunker pants. I ran up the stairs to my locker and threw on a uniform. I slid the pole down to the apparatus floor and grabbed my bunker gear. Lieutenant Tom Coleman made an announcement over the loud speaker requesting anyone who owned a handheld police/fire scanner to bring it. I told him I had a cellphone—it was still a novelty item at the time and I thought it might be helpful.

There was an industrial tool supply store across the street from the firehouse and Lieutenant Coleman and a bunch of the guys asked them for tools and a truck. We grabbed shovels, crow bars, power saws and anything else that might help us rescue the thousands of people we were sure were going to need saving. While we were loading the truck I noticed a handful of people—ghosts really—walking up Hamilton Avenue. They were coated in dust and all had the same blank stare on their faces. I went over to one woman. Her hair was white with a chalky coating of dust and black gunk crusted the bottom of her eyes.

"Do you need to use our phone?" I asked. She did not answer. She didn't even look at me, but kept walking.

"Do you need to wash up?" I added. Neither she nor the other stragglers responded. They must have walked through the Battery Tunnel, an under-river tube nearly two-miles long.

A dozen or so men piled in the back of the white box truck with the tools. A man in a blue windbreaker came toward us and flashed a badge.

"I'm a federal agent," he told us. "You guys heading in?"

The federal agent climbed into the cab and I squeezed into the middle next to the driver, Gary Kakeh.

"You guys might not want to sit there," said Gary. "They may see an Arab driving a stolen delivery truck and open fire."

The agent and I laughed. Gary was the senior man in Ladder 131. He was a Vietnam veteran who grew up not far from the firehouse. Gary loved to joke about everything, including his family's Arabic background. We knew the Battery Tunnel would be closed so we drove to the Brooklyn Bridge—the BQE was deserted and we arrived in lower Manhattan quickly. Emergency vehicles were everywhere and we had to park on Chambers Street.

We started walking, laden with power saws, shovels and crowbars—never imagining they'd be useless. A couple of blocks from the Trade Center I saw a massive black cloud come up the avenue ahead and turn down the street we were on. There was no loud noise to precipitate the ominous nebula that quickly overtook us. The street went from clear day to shadowy dusk and we were all coated with a layer of gray. Forward we went and arrived at a staging post at the intersection of two now unrecognizable streets. We put down the tools and

Lieutenant Coleman and the other officers went to find whomever was in charge.

None of us had handie-talkies. Each company was issued enough hand-held radios for the on-duty personnel—all of our radios were with the guys who were working that morning. Consequently, we had no sense of what was going on just a few hundred feet away from us. At the time we arrived, there were survivors inside the collapsed towers calling out for help. There were chiefs on scene, with radios, coordinating efforts. We were told to stand-by initially. An impromptu triage center was set up in a Duane Reade on the corner. I ran into one fireman I had worked with who told me how he narrowly escaped being crushed in the Trade Center parking garage. Another said that a fireman had been killed before the collapse when someone jumping from the upper floors had landed on him. A rumor was also circulating that a taxi had driven up to the command post and exploded. The fate of the second tower was still unclear. I thought someone had said it had collapsed as well. *Was it a partial collapse?* I wondered. *What was that dust cloud we walked into? Was it a secondary collapse?*

We were eventually assigned to the north side of the collapse zone and we started walking around the perimeter. On the corner was a short office building, maybe six stories tall, and the lower floors were on fire. Two firefighters were on the roof, leaning over the parapet and waving for help. Up ahead, I saw firemen run into the lobby only to return quickly as it was impassable. A tower ladder was quickly moved into position and people were scrambling to set the outriggers and raise the bucket. We all started clearing debris away to give the outriggers clearance. On the corner was Engine 155's rig. I had worked a training rotation in 155 and knew the chauffeur, Frankie Fontaino.

"Frankie, where are the boys?" I asked.

He worked furiously to attach a thick intake hose to the hydrant on the curb—not knowing that whatever water it held would soon run out as the water mains were all damaged in the collapse. He yelled back without turning toward me. "They're in there," he said, nodding toward the building on fire.

The two firefighters on the roof were at last brought down to the street safely. I caught sight of Will Hickey, whom I had worked with the year before. He was presently doing a training rotation in Ladder 105. He looked lost.

"Will—What's up?"

"Hey Andy," he answered, his expression blank.

"Where's 105?" I asked.

"I don't know. I was supposed to be there with them. Captain Brunton called me. He asked if I wanted to work overtime today."

Will was probably in his late twenties when he was hired by the Fire Department, but he looked like a teenager. He had a baby face and probably shaved once a week—tops. And so, I will never forget what he told me next.

"I stopped to shave. I shaved first before I left the house. When I was parking at the firehouse, the doors went up and the rig went out on the run. I missed them by a minute."

**

We continued around the perimeter. Walking straight was difficult as there was debris everywhere. I mostly looked at the ground before me to avoid tripping, but every so often looked over at the smoking mountain of mangled building to my right. The area involved seemed impossibly vast. At one point, I saw a man running out of the pile cradling something against his chest. He ran straight to where I was standing and I recognized him as Matty James. Matty was the Brooklyn trustee for the firefighters' union and he was not wearing bunker gear or a helmet. His dark hair was dusted white and he had tears running down his face. In his arms was a crumpled up American flag wrapped in a steel cable. He struggled to untangle the twisted dirty banner and somebody pulled a set of wire cutters out of their coat pocket. Before long the flag was free and though I don't remember anyone discussing strategy, a small team worked quickly to find a portable ladder and lay it up against the horizontal bar of a streetlamp. Two of us butted the ladder while Matty climbed up and fastened the flag to the lamppost—vertically with the stars on top and the stripes hanging down. It was the very antithesis of soldiers or astronauts planting a flag on some hard-fought hill or wondrous moonscape. It was a desperate grasp at meaning and control—the two things that felt most elusive. It was fleeting, but seeing the flag flying high filled me with pride.

I remember walking north toward Building 7, which was also on fire. I felt a hand on my shoulder and turned my head to see FDNY Commissioner Thomas Von Essen. He patted my shoulder and kept walking at a faster pace than us. We passed Building 7 to see multiple floors on fire—free burning and nobody was doing a thing about it. The city's Office of Emergency Management had been housed there and abandoned early on. I guess the chiefs knew it was evacuated and decided there were greater concerns at the moment. Again, we were told to standby. Every so often I would be near somebody with a handie-talkie and I could hear the chiefs struggling to implement some kind of system. Rescues were happening and I felt useless standing by. An impromptu staging area formed as the officers again peeled off to try and find direction.

We met up with other members of Engine 279 and Ladder 131. They had made it to the firehouse after us and arrived downtown later. Still, nobody knew anything about the guys who were on duty that morning. I looked at the massive smoking pile of twisted steel with a knot in my stomach. We were told to move back to West Street because Building 7 was expected to collapse. We used the time to talk about our guys. We went back and forth with who was working and where could they be. I thought about Mark Ruppert. He was opposite me on the chart, so we often traded tours to accommodate each other's schedule. I had asked him to work for me that morning so I could go to my college classes.

**

After several hours of burning, 7 World Trade Center collapsed. By that point we were joined by a few firefighters who were equipped with handie-talkies and we heard the immediate cacophony of transmissions as soon as the high-rise imploded. A fresh coating of dust and debris wafted down on everything in sight and multiple fires broke out in the surrounding area. We came down Greenwich Street, just north of where 7 had stood, to see a dozen or so cars on fire. The vehicles had been parked perpendicular to the curb outside some government office and now formed a neat row of flaming props waiting to be jumped over by some daredevil motorcyclist.

Chris Kielczewski, also of Ladder 131, and I popped the lock on an office building adjacent to the cars and headed for the stairwell. We took the fire hose in the cabinet next to the standpipe and unscrewed it from the outlet. Chris then grabbed the hose from the other stairwell and we joined them together, forming one long hose. I brought the nozzle outside and handed it off to a couple of engine guys and told them to standby while I ran back to Chris to tell him to start the water.

The office building we were in was quite tall, so the standpipe had easily thirty stories worth of head pressure from the water tank on the roof. Chris opened the outlet all the way and I ran back out to see how the engine guys were making out, wishing I had a handie-talkie to call them. What I saw outside was something out of a cartoon. The two men on the nozzle were being whipped around like ragdolls. Their feet were practically off the ground. I ran back to Chris and told him to cut back on the pressure and no doubt missed the engine guys cursing the damn truckies who don't know shit about standpipe pressure.

The cars were extinguished and tower ladders were backed down the block to pour water on the smoldering heap that was Building 7. We humped large caliber hoses long distances and were repositioned around the perimeter of the pile several times. The water mains were severed. Hydrants were dead and water had to be pumped from the Hudson River via fireboats. Faucets were dry. By now, our eyes were caked in dust and our throats were parched. We had seen people handing out water bottles earlier and Chris Kielczewski walked ahead to find something to drink and maybe clean our eyes with. He came back with two warm bottles of Corona and a handful of napkins. "It's all I could find," he explained as he poured the beer into the napkins to moisten them. He was handing me a beer and napkins when Chris Gaffney, also from 131, saw us.

"Look at this fuckin' guy," he said dryly. "Every dark cloud has a silver lining!"

We laughed and began wiping the dust out of our eyes with the wet napkins. Other guys came over and took off their fire hoods and poured the beer into the fabric so they could wipe out their eyes as well. Finally, somebody arrived with bottles of water and it took a few sips before my mouth and throat moistened again. We were west of the Trade Center near the West Side Highway and a large group of firefighters were now staged there. It was the late afternoon. Somebody called the firehouse and we found out that Lieutenant Gary Wood, who was 131's officer that day had checked in. Lieutenant Wood and the men of Ladder 131 had survived the collapse. Matty Castrogiovanni was in the hospital—the rest of the guys were banged up, but alive. Sean Halper, who was driving Engine 279 survived but nobody had heard from anyone else in the engine.

I was glad the guys from the truck all made it out. I thought about Mark Ruppert, who was working my shift. *How would I have felt if he had died?* I thought about the engine guys. *If they had gotten out they would have checked in.*

The officers walked ahead to talk to the chiefs and I saw Warren Forsyth, whom I'd worked with before. He was a gruff and salty veteran who spent most of his career in Rescue 1. He was boisterous and came from a big family of firemen. To a young guy like me Woody, as he was called, seemed larger than life. "Hey, Woody— what's up?" I asked, hoping he'd know something I didn't. He shook his head and turned back toward the smoking pile.

"We lost a thousand guys today," he said grimly.

I stared at the smoke rising and the pit in my stomach returned. *A thousand guys.* The number was unimaginable. *How many people were in the towers?* I wondered. *Ten thousand civilians must be dead.*

The officers returned. We were split-up by our work chart group numbers. Half were ordered to go off duty and come back to the firehouse in the morning. Until further notice, we would work 24 hours on, 24 hours off. The 279/131 guys who were ordered to go off duty (myself included) gathered up and walked back to the truck we had borrowed from the hardware supplier. En route we found Ladder 131's rig. It was parked on the West Side Highway and covered in debris. The windows were black with dust and the inside was completely filled with pulverized remnants of the Twin Towers. We looked inside. It was a disaster. Under the front seat was a thermal imaging camera—a new and expensive piece of equipment. Our captain, Marty Ford, took it.

**

We drove back to the firehouse in Red Hook. There was a group of people gathered in front. As I was walking in, a young man came over to me.

"Is Mike Ragusa here?" he asked.

I got choked up. Mike was 29 years old and short—the butt of many a joke, many of which were told by him. He was always working on his car, souping it up with new rims or some other detail, and he always, always had a smile on his face. He was working in Engine 279 that morning.

"He's not," I answered with a shaky voice. They were all Mike's friends. They had heard he was on duty and hadn't heard from him, so they gathered in the only place that made sense—Mike's firehouse.

"He was working today?" the young man asked.

I nodded. I didn't know what to say. I was pretty sure Mike was dead, but not positive. *What do I tell them?* I went inside and started taking off my bunker gear. To this day I wish I had said something more to Mike's friends.

After I showered, I saw Joe Thompson getting dressed. Joe had been off duty and in Midtown Manhattan when the attacks happened. He responded to a firehouse on the

West Side and was told to report to a staging area where he waited for hours before deciding to go back to his own firehouse to retrieve his gear.

"What's up, Joe?" I asked.

"Headin' over," he answered simply. Joe had 15 years on the job, if he said it was OK to go, that was good enough for me.

"I'll go with you," I answered.

Joe gave the crooked smile he usually reserved for dirty jokes, but instead of laughing he just finished getting dressed. As we were loading our bunker gear into Joe's car, Captain Ford came over with the thermal imaging camera.

"Take this," he said as he handed the heavy, pistol-gripped camera to me. The tool was a foot long with a boxed-out display screen on top. It produced an image of differences in surface temperatures and could see heat and fire through smoke as well as make out shapes of human bodies by temperature relative to the surrounding environment. The cameras were new to the department at that time and Ladder 131 had just received it days before. We had been training on the tool but hadn't really used it yet. It was so unfamiliar that Lieutenant Wood had left it on the rig when they arrived at the Trade Center. Thinking we may be able to see bodies under light rubble or stuck in dark voids, Joe and I thought it would be a good tool to have.

Captain Ford patted me on the shoulder and nodded the silent instruction of which I needed no verbalization. *Be careful.* He turned toward the stairs to tackle the administrative tsunami that I'm sure awaited him in his office.

**

We were driving to the worst disaster either of us could have ever imagined and five guys from our firehouse were missing—I'm sure we had a lot to talk about. I remember getting in the car with Joe, but for the life of me I have no recollection of what we talked about. Did we discuss the fact that our country was under attack? Did we talk about Mikey's friends camped out in front of the firehouse, or A-Rod's (Probationary Firefighter Anthony Rodriguez) baby due Thursday? What about Ronnie Henderson, the 20-year veteran and father of four? Did we talk about Christian Regenhard, the new guy in 131 who switched to work in the Engine that morning? How about the covering lieutenant whose name we didn't even know? I have no idea.

I remember parking somewhere just over the Brooklyn Bridge. Joe stuffed his FDNY parking placard in the window and locked up. His was the lone clean car in a row of anonymous dust-caked vehicles. I put my bunker coat on and gray dust billowed out of the fabric. I donned my helmet and we walked toward the bright lights and smoke. Security checkpoints were setup with barriers but no one stopped us. I'd had enough of staging areas that afternoon and we walked past the churning generators and spotlights, bypassing groups of guys awaiting orders from chiefs and went straight onto the pile. We crossed over twisted beams with no immediate goal in mind. There was a lot of smoke rising from the debris and we did our best to navigate around the worst of it. Lying open on the rubble in a desolate little valley we found two SCBAs (Self Contained Breathing Apparatus, the air packs worn by firefighters). They both had face pieces and a full tank of air. We spent no time questioning their abandonment as we each swung a cumbersome air pack onto our backs. It proved to be a fortuitous find.

We didn't completely don the face pieces—the cylinders held only 30 minutes of air and we wanted to conserve. We instead took intermittent hits of fresh air whenever the smoke got too bad. We tried to crawl into a few voids but they all seemed to be dead ends. The thermal imaging camera was useless. Scanning the pile showed nothing but the shape of hot, twisted beams; and aiming it into voids proved just as pointless. Furthermore, it was bulky to carry and I wished I hadn't brought it. A little further ahead we saw a small group of firemen taking turns digging under a large section of steal—among them was Danny Conniff. Years before, Danny and I had been truck drivers together—both of us on the firefighters' list waiting to be called. He worked in Ladder 108 and I would run into him from time to time. We made eye contact.

"What's up Dan?" I asked with a nod.

"Hey—And... What's up?" he shot back before coughing forcefully into the bend of his arm.

I raised the face piece that was dangling from its air hose and offered him a hit of air. He refused. I don't remember if we said anything after that. What was there to say? Joe and I moved on—trying to find crawl spaces and voids where we might find somebody trapped. The steel was so tangled, so compacted that it seemed hopeless, until we came across a battalion chief standing next to a company of enginemen. The lieutenant was talking to the chief; two firefighters stood to the side with a charged, 1 ¾" hose line. The nozzleman held the tool of his trade firmly out front with the control handle shut. I looked behind them to see where the hose line was coming from. I couldn't tell. I remember thinking then— and I still feel so today—that it must have been some feat of determination to stretch a charged 1 ¾" line over hundreds of yards of jagged, hot steel and smashed concrete. Their water source was an even bigger mystery. Presumably, they were hooked up to a manifold (a distributor fed by a large hose which supplies multiple smaller diameter hoses) run off a line charged by a fireboat in the Hudson River. They worked their asses off to get that hose line in place. Their reaction to the chain of events that was about to unfold was completely understandable.

The chief saw Joe and I with SCBAs on our back and turned to the lieutenant.

"Give them the hose line," he directed.

"This is *our* line, Chief," answered the engine company's boss, forcefully but respectfully.

"I'm not sending your guys down there without masks," answered the chief, with equal force. He looked over at the nozzleman. "Hand it over."

The lieutenant was furious. I didn't make eye contact with the nozzleman as I took hold of the nozzle. I would have been beside myself if I were in his shoes. This was a huge breach of etiquette and tradition. The chief was communicating, via handie-talkie, with a command post and with somebody somewhere below us—he had a lot on his plate and he was trying to solve logistical problems as quickly as they arose. It probably didn't dawn on him to ask Joe and I to give our SCBAs to the engine guys and assign us to back them up. I didn't care. I was so desperate to do something positive—make some sort of difference—that I jumped at the chance to take control of the line without ever wondering where we were bringing it. Clearly it was someplace too dangerous to be without an SCBA.

The chief told us quickly that there were members at the bottom of a tunnel extricating a trapped policeman (who I would learn later was Sergeant John McLoughlin of the Port Authority Police Department) and the operation was being impinged by fire burning at the bottom of an elevator shaft at the base of the void. The opening was small and unremarkable—just a narrow space between twisted steel. I looped the stiff and heavy hose around to face the right direction and lowered one foot into the crevice. I looked back to see Joe right behind me. The chief was a few steps back, talking on the radio. The thing that strikes me most—now, over 16 years later—is how few people were there at the void's opening. If that had been any other rescue happening at any other incident, there would have been dozens of people. Rescue personnel and equipment would have been staged all around, ready to be rotated into the operation at a moment's notice. But there at the scene of the greatest manmade disaster to strike our city—where hundreds of people were looking for something to do just a few dozen yards away—there was just one battalion chief at the top of the hole.[†] Clearly the rescue was being directed from afar. After all, somebody had ordered that engine company to stretch the hose line. I would later learn that this particular rescue operation had been going on for hours and that one Port Authority police officer had already been extricated and transported to the hospital.[‡] The desolation I felt, however, as I crouched to

---

[†] The number of rescuers staged at the entrance to the void fluctuated throughout the night. Based on accounts from rescuers I interviewed, there was a slightly larger grouping of responders earlier and—as I will soon show—a much larger group later. However, when Joe and I descended into the void there was only the one battalion chief and the engine company that gave us the hose line.

[‡] Rescuers of the first Port Authority police officer pulled from void, Will Jimeno, include former Marines Dave Karnes and Jason Thomas, paramedic Chuck Sereika, Detective Scott Strauss, Firefighter Tom Asher, and others. Jimeno was removed first and work continued on McLoughlin with rescue personnel being rotated in and out. Among them were Firefighter Joe Esposito and Lieutenants Tony Errico and John Kiernan. As this book is intended as a memoir and not a

crawl into the void—the ostensible smallness of the operation—bespoke the insanity of the first hours after the attacks. I looked down at my watch; it was twenty-five minutes to midnight.

It was dark on that section of the pile and inside the void was darker, but there was just enough faint light that we could see what we were crawling on. After a straight drop of about five feet into which Joe and I had to sit on our asses and shimmy down, the path tightened to a skinny ramp-like corridor. To my left was a steep drop off that went straight down at least 20 feet. The whole space was only about three feet wide but the ramp we were crawling down was about a foot wide. It descended sharply. To my right was twisted steel and small pockets of empty space. Gray dust was everywhere. I had to go slowly to keep my knees from sliding off the ramp and to give Joe a chance to feed me hose line, which kept getting caught behind us. The SCBAs on our backs were bulky and it was awkward maneuvering around the protruding steel on our right.

The proverbial light at the end of this treacherous tunnel was an officer's light held by Battalion Chief Robert Stock, who was the commander of the 32nd Battalion in Brooklyn—my battalion. He knelt in a clearing about five feet wide and three feet high. To his right was the bottom half of an elevator's hoistway doors. Smoke was seeping out of the doors' seams and filling the clearing. Across from us a massive steel beam dissected the clearing in two. I could not see around it. Popping out from under the beam was a torso.

Chief Stock explained our mission while I stared down at the backside of this body smashed into halves and

---

complete history, I have focused on the operation only after my arrival.

pinned. It was a man, facing the other way. His hair was coated in flaky white dust. His shirt had lapels—he was a cop. I figured he was high ranking because his shirt was white. The chief put his hand on my shoulder and pointed to the elevator shaft.

"It's burning at the base," he said. "The smoke is endangering the guys on the other side."

Other side? I wondered as I followed Chief Stock's gaze. To the left of the pinned officer—under the giant beam that had killed him—was an opening. There was only about eight inches height and maybe eighteen inches width of clearance, but a small team of rescuers had made their way under toward a police officer pinned on the other side—alive.

The chief backed around Joe and I so we could get near the elevator. I edged into position, on my knees next to the dead officer. Smoke rose from the space between the hoistway door and the platform before it. I pushed in on the doors and they swung into the shaft creating a large opening at the bottom. I could not see how far down the shaft went—it was completely dark inside and smoke billowed quickly into the large space I had just given it. I let the door swing closed and put my face piece on. I sucked in a big gulp of fresh air and mashed my helmet down over the face piece's straps. Again I pushed the elevator door in and I pointed the nozzle into the shaft. I opened the control handle and the kickback pushed my body back into Joe's. He steadied me from behind. The sound of crashing water and the deep mechanical snoring of my air mask were the only sounds I could hear. Within 30 seconds the chief was whacking me on the shoulder. I knew what this meant and immediately shut the nozzle. The elevator door swung closed and I pulled off my face piece.

"The water's backing up into the void," yelled the chief.

I looked down and saw what he meant. Water was seeping from the far side of the massive beam and puddling around us. The rescuers on the other side had called out to tell the chief to stop the water. I looked around. *How the hell is it backing up in here?* I wondered. I had been pointing the stream directly down the shaft. I pushed the door in again. Smoke pushed up and I surveyed the options quickly and then let the doors swing back. I adjusted my angle and opened the nozzle again. Within a few seconds the guys on the other side started screaming. I shut it down.

"Try venting the smoke out one of the openings," said the chief.

Joe and I spun the clumsy hose line around and backed it up the narrow ramp—about half way back to the entrance point. I screwed off the outer tip of the nozzle to create a wider stream and pointed it out one of the openings between the twisted steel. In structural fires, we often use this method to clear a room of smoke. Once the actual fire is extinguished, a wide nozzle stream can be directed out a window to create an airflow behind it—sucking out the smoke with it. I didn't have a window to work with, however. The space I directed the stream through was small and above our head pointing up. I couldn't see the outside world through it, but instead worked on faith that an opening about this far down in the void might go up into fresh air. I opened the nozzle.

I can only imagine what it must have looked like up on the pile above us—this geyser coming out of nowhere. No matter, the stream had no effect on the smoke inside the void and what's more, water was once again pooling on the ground below. After a minute, the chief told us to shut the line down. We were just going to have to live with the smoke. We lay the hose line down on the ramp and committed the engineman's cardinal sin of abandoning it.

Joe and I took off the SCBAs. It was too tight down in the clearing to wear the bulky masks. The smoke was a nuisance, but not overpowering at the moment. The fire was confined to the base of the elevator shaft and the closed elevator doors deflected most of it. The chief, the rescuers under the beam, and most importantly the trapped policeman, didn't have SCBAs. I figured it was best to conserve the air we had in case the smoke got worse. We awkwardly slipped out of the mask straps, not having enough room to extend our arms. I shoved the SCBA into a space between twisted beams and tucked the face piece and air hose around it. It had been my ticket in, but now our roles were shifting.

Joe and I kneeled beside the chief at the base of the clearing. If the guys on the other side of the beam freed the policeman, they would have to pass him out to us. The problem—as far as I could tell—was that a concrete slab lay across the lower half of the cop's body. There was no room for pneumatic air bags or any other kind of rescue device we would normally have used to lift the slab. There was no way to get a power tool above to break the concrete. The rescuers dug around the cop's body by hand hoping to create enough space to wiggle him free without much luck. Little was said between Joe, the chief, and I. We waited patiently for either good news from under the beam or at least a request for help of some kind: a tool—anything. The chief kind of squatted on some steel to give his handie-talkie as straight a line as possible out of the hole, and Joe was directly behind me, leaving me directly beside the dead police officer pinned under the beam.

I wanted to know something about him. I put my hand on his shoulder and, to my surprise, dust puffed up revealing the shirt's true color—dark blue. He wasn't a high-ranking officer; he was a cop. He had shown up for work that morning like so many others, opened his locker and put on his uniform. *What was he thinking about when he got dressed? His family? His passions?* I pulled his shoulder toward me slightly to look at him. His face was dirty, but he could have been sleeping. I couldn't see a nameplate but his badge was there. 'Port Authority Police' it said proudly. It was still shiny even in the dim, shadowy light. I thought about his family. At that moment, they didn't know he was dead. I knew something the people who loved him most didn't. That bothered me and the first thought that came to mind was to take his badge. *I'll bring his badge to his family*, I thought. *At least they'll have his badge to hold on to.* A second later I realized that that was a terrible idea. *He's here. His badge should stay with him. He will be extricated eventually and his badge will ensure he's identified and both he and his badge will be reunited with his family.*

I let go of his shoulder and I didn't disturb him again.

A good hour must have passed and the chief's radio crackled with word they were sending a fresh team down to relieve the men under the beam.

"Send out Rescue 4 and I'm sending down Squad 270," said some tinny voice.

"Rescue," the chief called out. "You guys are being relieved."

The fact that there was no argument from the guys from Rescue 4 bespeaks the exhausting nature of the work. One at a time, three men from Rescue 4 slid out on their bellies from under the beam. It was by no means easy to wiggle out and each man needed help righting himself on our side. They were sweaty, filthy, and utterly spent. I recognized Firefighter Liam Flaherty, the leader of the Emerald Society Pipes and Drums band that played bagpipes at every FDNY funeral. I'd seen him at funerals in the past and would see him at scores more in the coming months. He was joined by Firefighters Bill Murphy and Ed Morrison. "We basically worked until we couldn't see anymore," [29] remembered Morrison, describing how irritating the smoke was to his eyes after hours in the void. Though he was a veteran rescue specialist, the punishing conditions left Morrison hardly sanguine. "Holy shit!" he recalled thinking. "How are we going to get him out?"[30] The next crew would need to continue the painstaking work exactly where Rescue 4 left off. Flaherty, Murphy, and Morrison wearily ascended the jagged ramp and gave detailed instructions to the men relieving them. It was now Squad 270's turn to crawl under the beam into the tiny opening.

I didn't know them at the time but would later learn they were Firefighters Don Schneider and Mike Smithwick, and Lieutenant Doug Sloan. Also with them was Firefighter Tommy Bohn, who would at one point swap places with Schneider only to swap back when Bohn's husky frame proved too bulky for the tight space.

The guys from Rescue 4 had described how far they'd gotten and what they thought needed to be done. It didn't sound good. *How the hell are they going to get him out by hand?* The men from 270 went to work and Joe and I waited. Chief Stock was eventually called up for relief and another battalion chief took his place.

For hours we waited—hours kneeling with the rising smoke and the dead policeman. We waited for a chance to *do* something. We could hear the guys on the other side of the beam. They dug by hand, tried shifting some stuff, and dug some more. But they never called back for our help. The pace was agonizingly slow and the space in which to work impossibly tight. The smoke hadn't stopped rising and from somewhere in the debris, a PASS alarm was ringing. The Personal Alert Safety System, or PASS, is a monitor attached to firefighters' SCBA which—

once activated—rings if kept motionless for 30 seconds. It works as a beacon should a firefighter become unconscious. Its alarm is high pitched and piercing. I had no idea where it was coming from but it was annoying and added to the tension. In any other situation, a ringing PASS alarm would cause us to stop whatever we were doing and search for the source. The situation at the bottom of that tight void, however, was a world unto itself. Where was it coming from? Nobody knew. What was it coming from? Everybody knew. Somewhere in the tangled hell, a fireman had been crushed and his PASS somehow survived well enough to now start ringing. The sound was echoing into our void but emanating from somewhere else. It was for others, up top, to find the source. We had a policeman pinned down here for almost a full day to worry about. Still, the sound was unnerving.

"I had used a Sawzall to cut away some aluminum studs covering his legs, but it was so tight I ended up ripping up my arm," Schneider would later tell me.[31] After a few hours, it was clear that the punishing conditions had taken their toll on 270 as well. They were ordered out. Physically exhausted and sick from the dust and smoke, Schneider vomited upon climbing up out of the hole and had to be taken to the Engine 10/Ladder 10 firehouse across Liberty Street for medical treatment.[32] This was disheartening. The squads and rescues are the most highly trained companies in the FDNY—all assigned members are collapse and technical rescue specialists.§ *If Rescue 4 and Squad 270 couldn't get him out, how bad must it be under there?*

I felt useless. It seemed like those making the decisions above were running out of ideas. What's more, I think

---

§Rescue and squad companies are part of the Special Operations Command, or SOC.

they forgot that Joe and I were down there. They never called us out to rotate fresh men in—which was fine with me. I wanted nothing else at that moment than to help somehow. As far as I was concerned, at the bottom of that smoky hellish void the most important thing in the world was going on. I didn't need relief, or rest, or fresh air. I needed to contribute.

The men from 270 had gone out and the chief received word that the next team would be from Ladder 111. Ladder 111 was not a SOC company and I remember thinking that if the next guys going under could do so without specialized training, then why couldn't I.

"Chief, I'm tall and skinny," I said while we waited for 111 to make their way down. "Maybe my long arms can reach around and dig out behind him."

The chief looked me over. "How much do you weigh?"

"One seventy," I answered—giving myself a ten pound discount.

Whether he knew I was fudging or not, he nodded. "If 111 can't get him out, you two will be next."

I don't know what made me think I would have better luck than Rescue 4, Squad 270 or 111 Truck, but I was convinced that if I could just get my hands in there somehow, it would work out. I took off my bunker coat to make myself as thin as possible. If I got the nod, I was going to be ready.

The guys from 111 arrived. I knew their faces but would only later learn their names: Firefighters Chris Eysser and Billy Reid, and Lieutenant Fred Mallett. Around the same time, the chief received word that medical personnel up top were worried about the possibility that McLoughlin was developing Crush Injury or Crush Syndrome.** They were sending down medics to try to get an I.V. on the patient. I could see on the chief's face what he thought about our chances of getting an I.V. in, but he kept his opinions to himself. Down the ramp came a paramedic/NYPD Emergency Service Unit (ESU) officer.

It would not be until years later, after reading an article in the *Journal of Emergency Medical Services,* that I would learn the full extent of the drama unfolding regarding Sergeant McLoughlin's medical condition during the hours of extrication. At the top of the hole, an emergency medicine resident and former paramedic named John Chovanes and Detective John Bushing, a paramedic himself, were monitoring John McLoughlin's condition. At various times during the extrication, the two men rotated down into the void to monitor the patient's vital signs and administer oxygen and morphine. Somehow, they got an I.V. into the patient. When they returned to the surface, they worked out a detailed plan to amputate both of John McLoughlin's legs mid-thigh.[33] The situation was becoming desperate.

Also rotated into the void was a Nassau County ESU cop, Richard Doerler. The clearing on the near side of the beam was now crowded. Under the beam, conditions were even more cramped and the rescuers had to contort their bodies to reach behind McLouglin's legs where the

---

** The American College of Emergency Physicians defines Crush Injury as the "compression of extremities or other parts of the body that causes muscle swelling and/or neurological disturbances in the affected areas of the body," and Crush Syndrome as "localized crush injury with systemic manifestations. These systemic effects are caused by a traumatic rhabdomyolysis (muscle breakdown) and the release of potentially toxic muscle cell components and electrolytes into the circulatory system."
(www.acep.org/MobileArticle.aspx?id=46079&parentid=740, 2/24/18).

digging needed to happen. Doerler would later describe how he had to straddle McLoughlin's body to be able to barely reach small bits of debris with his left hand—even though he's right-handed.[34]

"After digging for hours with little hand tools, I was finally able to get some nylon webbing around his body and legs," Chris Eysser would later tell me. "I had to lay on top of his body to do it, but I was so glad to just get it around him."[35] He handed the webbing under the beam and Joe and I each grabbed a tail and wrapped our hands with the thin rescue strap.

We pulled on the webbing and McLoughlin let out a loud scream. There was shear agony in his voice; he didn't budge an inch. "Hold up," yelled back one of the rescuers. I let the webbing slacken in my hands and we waited. The chief looked down at his watch. "We gotta get him out," he uttered to us. He then called out to the guys under the beam for an update.

They answered that his legs were now accessible but they still couldn't free them from the slab. There was still no room for airbags; here is where the Fire Department's glacial speed at distributing new technology came into play. We carry a tool called a Hydra-ram, which is used for forcing open locked doors. Hydraulic fluid pushes a steel piston out and pops the door inward away from the jamb. New Hydra-rams had been circulating—nice self-contained units with a compact handle. Ladder 131, however, still had the old version of the Hydra-ram, known as a Rabbit Tool. The Rabbit Tool was a cumbersome, two-piece unit with a four-foot hydraulic line connecting the pump handle and the piston block. The entire tool was bigger and heavier than the new Hydra-ram, but the piston block—when cradled—laid flatter than the Hydra-ram (which had a handle jetting out the side). When Joe and I heard that there was access to the concrete slab, but little clearance for a tool, we looked at each other with the same idea in mind. "Rabbit Tool," we said to each other.

The chief asked the rescuers if a Rabbit Tool would work. "There's no room for the handle," someone yelled back.

"No—the old Rabbit Tool, with the hose," the chief answered.

"Maybe!"

The chief radioed for "An old-fashioned Rabbit Tool. Repeat, an old-fashioned Rabbit Tool—with the hose."

Quicker than I would have thought possible, an old-fashioned Rabbit Tool was handed down into the void.[††] "Maybe some chocks too, for cribbing," I said to the guy who handed me the Rabbit Tool. I passed the tool under the beam. From above, someone yelled down into the hole.

"You want some lumber—for cribbing? How big?"

"No," I yelled back. "Just some little chocks, like the ones on our helmets." I was describing the small wedges of wood firefighters stick in the elastic band around their helmets to have something handy to keep doors from closing behind them.

Almost instantly, I was pelted by a dozen or so wooden chocks. They rained down into the hole. "Enough!" I yelled back. I handed a few chocks under the beam to the rescuers on the other side. Joe, the chief, and I exchanged looks while we waited for news. Shortly after, someone yelled back that we were going to try again. Joe and I

[††]In his interview for this book, Chris Eysser stated that he recalled being handed a small pneumatic rescue tool (then in service in the FDNY and similar to a Rabbit Tool). While I am certain that a Rabbit Tool was requested, and Joe Thompson (phone interview, December 1, 2017) and I remember being handed a Rabbit Tool, it is difficult, after so many years, to be 100% certain whose memory is correct.

grabbed hold of the webbing. On the other side of the beam, Chris Eysser prepared John McLoughlin for what was about to come. "John, you're almost there. It's gonna hurt like a bitch but then you're free,"[36] he told him. I heard the rescuers talking to McLoughlin about his four kids. They all seemed to be preparing him for one more push.

The chief grabbed my arm. "He's gotta come out this time," he said quietly.

I pulled the webbing, hand over hand, and McLoughlin let out another scream. At last, he was freed—his legs shooting out from the under the slab in what Fred Mallett described as "one quick pop."[37] The sergeant's screams tailed off as the rescuers on his side shouted encouragements. His head became visible under the beam—his hair caked white with dust. Next came his shoulders and I was surprised to see he was wearing a bunker coat (Port Authority cops were trained to act as a fire brigade at PA locations). The webbing straps shortened in my hands as we pulled him fully under the beam, but the clearing on our side was not wide enough for his outstretched body. We curled up his shoulders and I held him in my arms while a Stokes stretcher was worked in behind Joe and me.

"You're almost there John," I said. "You're gonna see your four kids soon."

The Stokes stretcher didn't fit in the clearing either—just the end of it was wedged under McLoughlin's shoulders. The rest of the stretcher was pointing up the jagged ramp. Joe and I leaned forward and grabbed hold of the cop's gun belt. Two sets of hands were pushing from the other side of the beam as the rescuers pushed McLoughlin forward with everything they had. The grueling hours had taken their toll. Mallet recalled being so physically spent by this point that he wondered if they'd be able to get the officer into the stretcher. "Chris [Eysser] just put his arms under the cop and lifted," Mallet remembered.[38] McLoughlin let out one final moan as we manhandled him into the stretcher, rougher than we would have liked but the only way possible. He was in the stretcher. After nearly a full day being buried, he was getting out of that hellish hole.

There were two people above the Stokes and they grabbed the top and Joe and I held it from the bottom. We worked the stretcher up the ramp and to the drop near the opening. The two men at the head climbed out and numerous hands reached in to grab hold of the stretcher. It was pulled out of our hands and out of the void for good. Joe and I went back down the ramp to get our gear.

One by one the rescuers gathered their things and headed out. It was tight—there was still the smoke and that goddamned PASS alarm—but nobody seemed to mind. I patted guys on the shoulder as they went past me and said, "Nice job," more than once. I said it because that's what we say—*Nice job.* It's about the only compliment firemen ever give each other, but that's not to say it's meaningless. In fact it is a very high compliment. It's what I said because it was what I knew, but it didn't do those guys justice. From the time Joe and I got down in that void, over eight hours before, I witnessed nothing but bravery and dogged determination. The guys from Rescue 4, Squad 270, Ladder 111, and that Nassau County cop pulled off the impossible.

"Why don't you guys just leave your stuff for now?" said the chief to Joe and me. "Go up and take a blow—let everyone get out of the way here and then come back for it."

My dusty, sweaty arm got stuck in the sleeve of my bunker coat as I continued dressing unchecked. "With all due respect, Chief," I answered. "I'm never coming down this fucking hole again."

The chief laughed. "I guess you're right," he said. Once my arm was fully in the sleeve, he patted me on the shoulder. I followed Joe up the ramp. Rays of daylight shone through the hole at the top and helping hands seemed to stretch down from 360 degrees.

I grabbed a hand and was pulled up to the surface. The desolate scene I had witnessed the night before—the lone battalion chief manning the hole—was a completely transformed landscape. There were now hundreds of people surrounding the hole. Some were clapping, many were crying. Lines of people stretched hundreds of yards back across the twisted steel. Hands reached out to help me walk over the debris. I was pulled in for a few hugs. My eyes watered up.

The people around the hole weren't just New York police and firefighters. They wore emergency workers' uniforms and gear from all over. Some wore medical clothing and others hardhats. The full scale of the tragedy fell upon me. Those clapping and those crying were sharing what the entire nation felt that morning.

It remains one of the most profound moments of my life.

CHAPTER 4

AFTER WE CLIMBED OUT OF THE HOLE, Joe and I went back to the firehouse in Red Hook. I showered and passed out in the bunkroom. I woke up a couple of hours later. For a moment I didn't know where I was and when I recognized the bunkroom I had the most unbelievably confusing sensation that I had just dreamt the attacks. For a full minute I lay there trying to decipher if it were real or a dream. I shot out of bed and went into the kitchen. On the TV was news footage of the smoldering ruins of the World Trade Center. *It was real.*

A bunch of guys were in the kitchen—still no word from Engine 279. We needed a plan. We wrote the names of each of the four firefighters missing on the chalkboard—as a chart. The officer, who we now knew was Lieutenant Anthony Jovic, had only recently been promoted from Ladder 34. He was covering in Engine 279 for just that day and had stepped into the firehouse just minutes before they received the run. Gary Kakeh called Ladder 34 and asked to speak with their senior member. He explained the situation with Lieutenant Jovic and offered our assistance with as much or as little share of the weight as desired in looking after the Jovic family. Knowing that we lost four other guys, Ladder 34's senior man's response was in keeping with typical firehouse spirit. "We got it, brother," he said and for the moment, we put all of our attention on the other four families.

HENDERSON. Ronnie lived upstate near Newburgh, not far from Gary Kakeh's home. Gary would contact and visit the Henderson family. *RODRIGUEZ.* Anthony lived on Staten Island—Kevin Dillon volunteered to visit them. *RAGUSA.* Mikey was from Brooklyn. Gerry Sweeney, who lived on Long Island signed up. Finally, the name *REGENHARD.* I looked at Christian's last name in block letters and tried to remember where he lived. He had either just moved or was about to move to Sunset Park, but he was single. *Where do his parents live?* I wondered. It didn't matter—I grabbed hold of the chalk and wrote my name.

We put lines across the chart with dates and times and decided that each family would be visited every day until we had more to tell them. There was no discussion of it, no vote. Gary, Kevin, Gerry, and I would become the firehouse contacts for these families. Right there in the kitchen a rudimentary system for taking care of the families was born—scrawled across the chalkboard. Under the time slots on our chart, other members would sign up by the day to assist by either visiting or making some other necessary accommodation. I went to the Ladder 131 office and looked up Christian's emergency contact number. I closed the door and dialed the phone with a lump in my throat. *What the hell am I going to say?*

An answering machine picked up and a young woman's voice spoke:

Hello, you have reached the Regenhard family. We don't have any information about Christian right now, but if you'd like to leave a name, number, and reason for calling, somebody will get back to you.

Beeeeeeeeeep.

"Um—Hello. My name is Andrew Serra. I'm from Christian's firehouse. I was calling to..."

"Hello," the same young woman broke in frantically.

"Hi, I work with Christian and..." I suddenly remembered just how desperate Christian's family must be and that I should not string her along. "I have no information on Christian," I said in as steady a voice as I could muster. I didn't want to get anybody's hopes up. "I just wanted to reach out to his family."

"I'm his sister, Christina."

"Christina, we would like to come by. Where do you live?"

"Well, my mom lives in Co-op City, but everyone is here at my place—in Yonkers."

**

The kitchen—and the firehouse in general—was in complete disarray. Neither company had a rig. Both were still at the Trade Center crushed and covered in debris. The men who had started their 24-hour shift that morning (September 12) reported for duty with no apparatus to ride. Most were sent to a staging area, or central location acting as a depot for firefighters and equipment (the staging area for northern Brooklyn was Ladder 119's firehouse in Williamsburg), where they were rotated to the Trade Center on city buses. Those who finished their shifts that morning either hung around the firehouse to help organize things or walked over to the Battery Tunnel and hitched a ride to the Trade Center to spend their off day digging. Joe and I had gotten back late that morning after having spent the entire night in that hole. Captain Ford told us to shower and get some rest. It was now early afternoon. Gary, Kevin, and Gerry were probably making the same type of call I had just made. On the table were several aluminum trays—neighbors were already dropping off food. I told the few guys remaining in the kitchen about my call to the Regenhard family. "I'm heading up there now," I announced.

I had no idea what I would do or say when I got there but the one thing I was sure about was that I didn't want to do it alone. None of the guys in the kitchen had a lot of time on the job and I could tell they were hesitant. I looked around—waiting.

"I'll go," said a voice from behind me.

I turned to see Gus Rallis. He had only a few months on the job—in fact he got to Engine 279 the same time Christian was assigned to Ladder 131. I remember when he first introduced himself as Konstantine Rallis.

"Wow, that's a big name," one of the guys said to him. "Do you have a nickname?"

"Not really."

"Well, what do you like to be called?"

"Anything but Gus."

"OK, Gus."

**

Gus and I took my car—a black 1996 Saturn SL. It was a stick shift with roll-up windows and we cruised unimpeded on the practically deserted highways. We wore our blue work-duty uniforms and I remember thinking that we should have worn our dress uniforms. Normally, the department sends a chief and a chaplain to make the first visit with a fallen firefighter's family. But hundreds of guys were missing—these were not normal times. Gus and I were making it up as we went along.

Gus didn't say much. I found out later that he was supposed to be working in Engine 279 on the morning of September 11. It was his scheduled tour but Christian had asked him to switch because he had dinner plans that evening. That is the reason Christian (assigned to Ladder 131) was working in Engine 279. We switch our tours all the time—it's called a Mutual Exchange of Tours, or just a 'mutual.' Veteran firefighters accepted this and had the feeling that once you traded tours with someone, *that* was your tour. If something happened during that tour, it was meant to be. Gus was still new and perhaps couldn't wrap his head around that. Who's to say anyone could? It had bothered me when I heard Mark Ruppert was caught in the collapse. How would I have felt if he had died? I think the first few weeks after the attacks were especially tough for Gus.

Sometime after Engine 279's rig was recovered, the daily riding list for September 11 was found. Riding lists are usually clipped to a rig's dashboard and show the members working in that company for the given tour. In addition to listing the names of the men who died, this riding list had the name *Rallis* written in and then crossed out. *Regenhard* was written beside it. The riding list was just another reminder of how random it all was. It could have been any of our names scribbled in.

If Gus was struggling with survivor's guilt, he wasn't alone. Sean Halper had been the engine chauffer on September 11 and drove the company there. He had pulled around the block to find a hydrant and was attempting to supply the standpipe system when the collapse occurred and was the lone survivor from 279. Sean was one of the senior members of the engine and our firehouse had faced tragedy before. Twelve years earlier, Firefighter John Devaney of Ladder 131 was burned to death while searching for trapped occupants in an apartment fire on Van Brunt Street. Devaney's loss—and the experience of putting a firehouse back together after such a tragedy—shaped the character of the senior men of Engine 279 and Ladder 131. In many ways, it laid the groundwork for the organization of the firehouse's response to 9/11. The problem was that the scale of the loss on 9/11 was unprecedented. The firehouse's organization would strain under such pressure and in other circumstances would have been bolstered by neighboring fire companies. After the World Trade Center attacks, however, there were no neighboring companies that weren't dealing with the same thing themselves.

On the afternoon of September 12, however, all of those things: Gus and Sean's struggle with guilt; the weight of the firehouse's loss; and the strain to rebuild and carry on; remained vague unknowns. We were aware of their inevitability but still dealing with the shock of yesterday's events. Gus, for his part, rose to the occasion. He and Christian had gone through the Academy and been assigned to the firehouse together. Christian was working *his* tour that morning. It could not have been easy for him, but here he was in the car with me. We picked up a few trays of take-out food from an Italian restaurant in the Bronx and drove to Christian's sister's house in Yonkers.

We rang the bell and were buzzed upstairs in the pre-war apartment overlooking the Bronx River Parkway. Gus and I squeezed into a rickety elevator more suited for a Haussmann flat than resembling anything Otis ever built here in the States. When we reached the apartment door, I looked over at Gus—holding the bag of food—and thought about what we might say. His look betrayed no greater insight than I had. *Nothing to do but knock.*

A young woman, about my age, answered and introduced herself as Christina, Christian's sister. I don't recall what I first said to her, but I remember looking over her shoulder into the apartment. A similar looking, but older, woman was mid-conversation with—judging by the cameraman setting up a shoulder-mounted video unit behind her—a woman I deemed to be a TV reporter. She stopped her conversation mid-sentence and excused herself with the reporter. She came straight over to Gus and me with her hand extended. I took her hand in mine and said nothing for a few seconds. Her eyes were watery, but she was otherwise composed. That was the first time I met Sally.

Chapter 5

Sally Regenhard worked in the public relations office of a large nursing home in Co-op City, the massive residential development in the north Bronx. She had also been an activist and member of the local planning board. In short, she knew how to organize a public relations campaign. By nightfall on September 11 and throughout the following day, many news outlets were reporting the unlikelihood of survivors in the rubble. Christian had spent five years as a Recon Marine; he had hiked and mountain-climbed his way across South America; he was no stranger to extreme adversity—if anyone could have survived it was Christian. The media may have been ready to give up on him, but they were about to slam up against a force of nature—Sally.

Quickly, she explained to me that the CBS news crew was working on a story about the families of the *missing* (not dead) and the anxious wait for news of their loved ones. Sally had spent her career gauging public opinion and dealing with politicians. She knew the time would come when the powers that be would want to turn the rescue effort into a recovery effort. She was not going to let that happen until every effort was made to reach anyone who might be trapped—alive. She asked me to say a few words on camera to let the public know that we, the firefighters, were not going to give up. My interview aired that night. I've never seen it and I have no recollection of what I said, but if I said that we were going to try like hell to find every survivor, I meant it. If I said I thought there were people trapped alive in voids waiting to be found and rescued, I believed it. After all, we had pulled John McLoughlin out alive that very morning. A woman was rescued that afternoon.

Maybe I just really wanted it to be true.

The news crew left and Gus and I were there with Sally, Christina, and a handful of family and friends. We didn't stay all that long. I didn't know what to say exactly. I told them we were doing all we could to find Christian and that if they needed anything to let me know. I told them I would be in constant contact with updates and... and...*What else could I say?* Before we left Sally hugged me. She now began to weep. I got choked up and through tears and a wavering voice I told her we were going to "dig until our fingers bled" and not stop until we found her son. I never imagined it would be a broken promise. I walked out of the apartment unaware of the significance of the meeting. Sally, Christina, and also Christian's father, Al, would become an integral part of my life for years to come.

**

I put on my bunker gear. It smelled. I have never been able to totally pinpoint the smell exactly. It was a mixture of concrete dust, burning flesh, and God knows what else. I didn't even have my spare bunker gear—it had been picked up a couple of days before September 11 for cleaning and had not come back yet. I put on the smelly gear and walked over to the Battery Tunnel. I was given a ride through by Triborough workers in the back of a pick-up truck and I walked up West Street to the site. The size of the operation had grown considerably. The scale of the collapse zone was already huge but now the surrounding blocks were filled with trailers and heavy equipment. There were tables set up giving out work gloves, dust masks, and bottled water. In front of one of the tables I saw Anthony Laieta, whom I had played Little League with. Anthony was a police officer and when I saw him I reached out my hand to greet him giving little thought to what I was saying,

"Hey, Anthony—what're ya doing?"

His face was stern and his eyes expressionless. "Looking for my brother," he answered.

"Vinny's here?" I answered mindlessly. "Where is he?" I looked around expecting to see Anthony's brother somewhere in the crowd.

"He worked in the Trade Center."

It was like a punch in the stomach. "I'm really sorry."

Anthony reached out his hand again and we shook. "I gotta get going," he muttered and walked away.

The operation was more organized now and it seemed like the chiefs had a system worked out for who would search what areas. I moved onto the pile and looked for some way to help. I was ushered onto a bucket brigade. Somewhere up ahead, guys dug into a void or under some beam and the debris removed was scooped into five gallon buckets and passed back. All over the site, hundreds of firefighters, police officers, and civilian volunteers formed endless lines and grabbed full buckets to pass back and empty ones to pass forward. Most guys on the pile were on bucket brigades. There were, however, restricted areas that only members of the Special Operations Command were allowed to enter. These were particularly dangerous voids that required specialized training and equipment. I watched a few guys run a pre-run belay line through rappelling harnesses they were wearing and lower themselves down the face of a mangled steel cliff. They began searching hidden areas at the bottom of this massive cavity—with teetering sections of the tower's façade overhead up high. *If there are any survivors,* I thought, *that's were they'll be.* I didn't feel like I was doing much good on the bucket brigade. *I want to be one of those guys.*

**

The next few days were a repetitive cycle of visiting the Regenhard family, digging on the pile when off duty, and waiting at staging areas when on duty. We still didn't have our rig back. On either the second or third day, a company of volunteer firefighters from New Jersey backed their truck into our firehouse and was responding to emergencies in Red Hook. The Fire Department had given them a set of our handie-talkies and an FDNY lieutenant was assigned to respond with them. They were there for a few days and even helped extinguish a fire in a factory. Since we didn't have a rig—when we were on duty—we were usually sent to staging areas and rotated to the Trade Center site on city buses. It was a lot of waiting around. I hated it. I wanted to be on the pile— finding people, finding our guys. Companies were sent to these staging areas from all over the city. Once, out of frustration, I asked if we were the only company at the staging area who lost people. *Five of our guys are buried there somewhere,* I reasoned. *How can they make us just stand around?*

"We're not gonna throw *that* around," said Lieutenant Jim Butler of Engine 279. That's all he said, but it was enough. I knew exactly what he meant: *Everybody lost someone.* I felt ashamed for having asked. Lieutenant Butler was always kind and always fair, but his answer was blunt, final, and exactly what I deserved to hear. When you have three years on the job, sometimes it takes a senior guy to put you back in your place. For the most part, the senior men of Engine 279 and Ladder 131 did a good job of keeping the younger members grounded during that crazy time. Still, I just wanted to get back on the pile. Off-duty days were easier—nobody stopped you from just walking over.

By week's end, we had a spare rig. They sent us a 1980's model tower ladder, with an open roof over the crew cab. We liked riding in the open but the department had considered them a danger and phased the rigs out. This one, however, was put back into service just for us. The vollies (volunteer firefighters) went back to Jersey and we did our best to equip the tower ladder with the gear we had. They sent us six brand new SCBAs that were a completely different make and model than anything we had seen before, so that took some getting used to. But, all in all, we got the rig put together enough to go back into service.

I remember riding through the Battery Tunnel in the back of a Triborough pick-up one night and a few of us got to talking. "How are we ever going to fight a *regular* fire again?" we asked. After all, we had responded to the greatest fire emergency and disaster in the city's history. *A couple of rooms burning in an apartment building would be a piece of cake from now on.*

"There's no such thing as a *regular* fire," Gary Kakeh chimed in. "You always have to respect fire—things can change in an instant." Once again, with seniority came wisdom. A few weeks later, I would be reminded of Gary's words. I was on the roof of a burning brownstone when a report was given of somebody trapped on the top floor. I decided to descend the rear fire escape to see if I could get to the trapped person and I grabbed the top of the "gooseneck"‡‡ ladder to drop down the fire escape. As I swung my body (loaded down with bunker gear and an

---

‡‡A "gooseneck" ladder is a long and narrow, upside down U-shaped, ladder which bends over the exterior wall of a building and leads from the roof level to the top floor fire escape landing.

SCBA) around the thin rails and stepped onto the top rung of the gooseneck, my foot slipped off. My body dropped and my feet swung out, dangling over a four-story drop to the rear yard. The only thing that saved me was the firm grip I had (with both hands) on the rails of the gooseneck. The senior men of Ladder 131 had taught me to always firmly grip the gooseneck's railing with both hands before putting your weight on the top rung. This was not a collapsing skyscraper that almost killed me. It was a four-story brownstone. Gary was right, *there's no such thing as a regular fire.* Anyway, Ladder 131 was back in service.

Around this same time, Engine 279 got their regular rig back. It had been covered in debris and caked—inside and out—in dust, but it wasn't too badly damaged. It was cleaned and put back in service. When the driver hit a bump, Trade Center dust billowed out of crevices in the dashboard and crew cab. On our on-duty days we were taking in runs in the neighborhood again. It felt good to resume this normal part of the job. That weekend, the funerals started.

A firefighter's funeral for a line-of-duty death is a ceremony steeped in tradition in which *every* firefighter (unless they are on duty) is expected to attend. It is not uncommon to have 10,000 firefighters, or more, lined up to salute the casket taking one last ride on a shiny fire truck as bagpipes echo up and down the line. There were a handful of firefighter funerals in the first few days. We were still working 24 on/24 off. We were spending our off-duty days either digging on the pile or visiting the families of our missing members. Now, we added funerals to the mix. By week two, the pace of funerals kicked into high gear and my life over the next couple of months went something like as follows.

My dress uniform was with me at all times. It hung on a hanger in the back seat of my Saturn. When I finished a 24-hour shift, I showered and put the uniform on. Local newspapers ran daily columns of all 9/11 related funerals happening in the tri-state area. If I was heading back to my home on Staten Island, I picked a funeral on the way to my house. There was almost always a funeral on Staten Island. I parked my car near the church, went and stood at attention for the procession in. There was then an hour of service inside the church. I usually only went inside the church if I knew the deceased personally (maybe 25 percent of the time). Other times I waited outside where loudspeakers played the service also. Then we lined up again for the procession out. It usually took about two hours, most of the time from around 11 am to 1 pm. Then I went home. By week two, we were working our normal chart again and half my shifts started at 6 pm. When that was the case, I went to one of the afternoon funerals on my way to work. There was scarcely a day when I wasn't either at the firehouse or at a funeral. Some days I did a morning funeral and an afternoon one. This was a shared experience. Everyone opened the paper and picked a funeral to stop at on their way home.

If I did stop home, it was usually just to check the mail and change out some laundry. I would then head back to the firehouse to grab gear and go to the site or head up to see the Regenhards—either at their apartment in Co-op City or at Christina's apartment in Yonkers. Al was also a former Marine and had spent 39 years with the Police Department, and Christina was a teacher, but like all of the 9/11 families, waiting for news and searching for answers took precedence over their former lives. I slept at the firehouse most nights; it was just easier. Those of us who were off duty—when we got back to the firehouse after being at the site—would sometimes shower and walk over to Lillie's, a small bar in the old section of Red Hook. A couple of hours with the guys over a few cold beers could work wonders emotionally. It was the only time we ever really talked things out. I'll never forget how Kevin Dillon described those first few weeks after 9/11 one night at the bar.

"When John died—it was a big deal," he said, speaking about John Devaney's death twelve years earlier. "The mayor came to the firehouse. The whole city had our back. But now, we lost five guys and we're on our own."

I was reminded of Josef Stalin's quote: "One death is a tragedy, a million deaths are a statistic." The individuals were being overshadowed by the numbers. In those first few weeks we were completely on our own. Much of the command staff at headquarters had been killed. The same was true for division commands and battalions. Whatever staff remained was dealing with the rescue and recovery operation at the site, the functional needs of staffing and equipping firehouses, and the multiple daily funerals happening across the five boroughs, Long Island, and counties north of the Bronx. A firehouse with members *missing* was—for the time being—left to their own devices.

I was making it up as I went along. I had no idea what I was supposed to be doing with the Regenhard family. Christian's body had still not been recovered, so there was nothing yet to do as far as a funeral was concerned. Christian wasn't married and had no kids, so there weren't practical matters to worry about like childcare or household maintenance. I decided that the best thing I could do for them was help them get through this terrible time with as much emotional support as I could give. I had no professional qualifications for such a task. I had some experience with loss, but I wasn't sure that it would apply to this most unique of situations. As it turned out, despite the vast differences of circumstances from one type of loss to another, the grief that is common to all those who lose a loved one is enough to build a relationship based on shared experience.

In the span of just a few years, my mother had lost her mother, her brother-in-law, and then her sister. As a teen-ager, I was given a front row seat to a succession of family tragedies that imbibed me with a keen sense of what the people closest to the deceased experience and need through such difficulties. My mother was a source of inspiration throughout these deaths as she seemed to know instinctively just how best to console others and turn her own grief into strength. Then, suddenly, my mother died. She was healthy one day and had a massive heart attack the next. She was 42 years old.

The death of my mother in my early twenties and 9/11 in my late twenties form the bookends of a long and difficult decade. I don't know if I believe in fate or in the idea that life gives us certain challenges to prepare us for still greater ones to come. What I will say is that the string of family tragedies and loss of my mother gave me a reservoir of emotional experience to draw from as I struggled to help the Regenhard family through an unimaginable abyss.

**

The pace of the funerals was now overwhelming. There were so many each day that it was hard to ensure a large turnout of off-duty firefighters to line up in the procession. The Fire Department had tried to spread the word to neighboring departments, but the effects weren't immediate. The strain was most visible about a month, or so, after the attacks. In the middle of one particularly busy week there was a memorial for a firefighter from my battalion, Thomas Kennedy of Ladder 101 at 4 pm out in East Islip, Long Island. Members of the 32nd Battalion were given a ride in a city bus that left from Ladder 101's quarters. We were standing in front of the church just before 4 and the fifty, or so, of us from the bus seemed to be the only people there. I remember looking around with a knot in my stomach. *How could this be?*

I was mortified. The Kennedy family was on the way to the church—they would be there shortly. Granted, the members of Engine 202 and Ladder 101 would be arriving with them, but that would still be only about a hundred firemen lined up. The minutes ticked away. We lined up—single file, not the usual six or eight deep—and made it barely to the end of the church. Everybody looked around, but I don't remember anyone saying anything about it. The senior guys put on a brave face and stared ahead. I fiddled with the tiny buttons on my white gloves.

Then, a yellow school bus turned onto the block and came to a stop right in front of us. The accordion door folded in clumsily and men in uniform—strange uniforms—started to file off. They were firefighters from Los Angeles. They looked around nervously, hoping they didn't miss it, I guess.

We started clapping. All of the FDNY members lined up gave the LA guys a big round of applause. It seemed like the thing to do. They had arrived just in time—fifty of them. They saw us clapping and began to weep. Fifty grown, burly men poured out the emotions of an entire nation. We began crying as well. Our formation broke down as each of us grabbed an LA fireman and hugged. They had come straight from JFK Airport—their luggage was on the school bus. We clapped for them and cried with them because they had saved us. We considered it a sacred duty to give the Kennedy family a proper line-of-duty funeral and just when it seemed hope was lost, these guys arrived. 9/11 touched all of America. These guys flew across the country, in their dress uniforms, to come help us carryout the duties we just could not handle on our own—we were overwhelmed. They saved us.

The LA guys lined up with us. Dozens of other firefighters arrived at the last minute and jumped on the end of the line. Our procession made it past the end of the block. It was very respectable. The Kennedy family turned the corner to see a solid line of blue uniforms leading to the church.

Word started to spread. Crowds at the funerals grew as firefighters from all over the country came to New York to pay respect to the fallen and, I think, participate in some way in what New York was going through. Everyone wanted to do something. Volunteers were no longer allowed to dig at the Trade Center site, access was much more strictly controlled. So visiting firefighters who wanted to help attended funerals. There were more and more to attend as time went by and families began to lose hope of recovering a body to bury and chose to have memorial services without a body. And some poor families held memorial services only to be told a month or two later that their loved one's body was now found. In these cases, sometimes the family would opt for a small burial service and sometimes they would feel the need for another funeral all together—reliving the nightmare.

All across the tri-state area, hundreds and hundreds of funerals inured a weary city to seemingly endless heartbreak. Bankers and brokers, guards and mechanics, dishwashers and waiters, cops and firemen: the dead came from all sections of society. Every neighborhood participated in the daily repetition of funerary rites. *The New York Times,* as well as many local papers, gave an obituary to every victim—giving faces to names and stories to statistics. Amid such loss, it was necessary to remind yourself of the individual stories. I remember one Saturday leaving the firehouse after an overnight shift and donning my dress uniform, as usual. I checked the newspaper for a funeral on my way home and hurriedly gulped down a cup of coffee as I ran out the door. It was at a church not far from my house on Staten Island. I parked a few blocks away and straightened my tie as I ran to jump on the end of the procession, just before the family and casket went by.

As I watched the antique fire engine creep forward with its American flag draped coffin atop the hose bed, I realized something horrible. I didn't know whose funeral I was at. I had run out of the firehouse in such a hurry to get to a funeral—to do something meaningful—that I forgot *what* the meaning was. I was so upset with myself that I vowed to never let that happen again. Going forward, I made it a point not to only know the name of the person whose funeral or memorial I was attending, but to learn something important about him or her. I would read the *Times'* obituaries and know the things that made that person special.

Of course, this wasn't an issue for my friends' funerals and memorials. Since none of the lost members of Engine 279 and Ladder 131 were recovered, there came a time for each of the families to have a memorial service. Funerals, in general, are never easy to plan. There is a litany of details that need tending. A Fire Department line-of-duty funeral (or memorial) comes with additional considerations: street closings to accommodate thousands of visitors; police presence for dignitary protection; transportation for not only family but dozens of firefighters from the firehouse involved; and of course—bagpipes. No Fire Department funeral would be complete without bagpipes and the FDNY Emerald Society's Pipes and Drums Band was stretched very thin in the months after 9/11. In normal times, most of this planning would be carried out by the Fire Department's Ceremonial Unit. But the convergence of 343 line-of-duty funerals and memorials meant firehouses were largely on their own to make these events happen.

Planning and executing four memorials (Lieutenant Jovic's service was planned by Ladder 34) was a difficult enough task. But perhaps more daunting was telling the families of the guys we lost that all hope was gone and the time to say goodbye was at hand.

CHAPTER 6

IN THE DAYS AND WEEKS following the attacks, I was visiting and/or calling the Regenhard family on a daily basis—Sally, Al, and Christina. They were dealing with not only the loss of their son and brother, but the not knowing. Initially, they hung fiercely to the hope that Christian was alive and days and even weeks hardly diminished this hope. It was, after all, not completely unheard of for survivors to be found in collapses weeks later—as long as there was somehow water. There were practical matters to attend nonetheless. We brought some of Christian's personal items—like a toothbrush and razor—over to a pier on the West Side where a DNA registry of all victims was being set up to help identify remains. Sally may have been hanging on to hope of finding Christian alive—a hope she fiercely protected—but she wasn't in denial. The pier was enormous and there had to be dozens of agencies set up with various registries. The missing and the dead were being organized into lists.

The irony is that I got to know the three surviving members of the Regenhard family far better than I ever knew Christian. I had only worked with Christian for a few months. We were friendly, of course, and I remember some conversations about his time in the Marine Corps and his travels in South America. We both turned 28 that August and I was drawn to his worldliness. I was surprised on an emergency call to the apartment of a Dominican family when Christian broke into conversation with the woman in fluent Spanish. I'm sure we would have become great friends in the succeeding months had he lived. But now, I was drawn by tragedy into the closest of relationships with Christian's parents and sister.

As with any family, the dynamics between individual members are diverse. Al was an old-time cop. In many ways, he and I spoke the same language. We were both fans of history and I found it very easy to relate with him. Though Christian was a free spirit who at first glance would seem more inclined to a Bohemian lifestyle than any kind of blue-collar job, he had followed his father's footsteps into the Marines and then civil service. Al must have been very proud to see his son don a uniform and I cannot imagine the heartbreak he must have felt losing him. Al's decades in the Police Department made him a realist and he confronted the tragedy with a detective's eye—compartmentalizing his grief, his anger, and his resolve.

Christina was a couple of years older than Christian (and me) but I came to feel like a big brother to her. She had just started a new job teaching science in a public school and the transition was now made all the more difficult by a family crisis that showed no signs of ending any time soon. Christian was still missing. In many ways the family's dilemma played out publicly as the search for survivors and then remains carried on and the nation turned its attention to the families. It was difficult for her to be in a brand new job—learning a challenging profession—while carrying the weight of her loss surrounded by coworkers and students who didn't know her. Her analytic mind and bookish wit gave me a welcomed outlet for conversation and temporary distraction.

If I had to choose one word to describe Sally it would be *fighter*. From the moment she heard of the collapse she was determined to use her grief and anger as catalysts for progress. In the months ahead she would found the Skyscraper Safety Campaign, an organization committed to improving safety codes in high-rise buildings. She would push local and federal lawmakers for change and fight for investigations wherever warranted. She would become a powerful spokeswoman for all of the families who lost loved ones on 9/11. But in the weeks immediately after the attacks, she would fight to get her son back. That meant pushing city officials to continue rescue efforts, It meant not allowing the bulldozers to sweep everything (remains and all) away once the sight was declared a recovery. I attended meetings with Sally for the families and I was always impressed at how efficiently she could organize action. She coped with Christian's loss by fighting for change and she rarely let her guard down.

There were times that the grieving mother came through—quiet moments and late night phone calls when Sally would break down. These were the times that left the greatest impression on me. The outside world showered the 9/11 families with a mixture of sympathy and curiosity, but only the families themselves know truly what it was like. Losing a loved one is a tragedy. Having your loved one murdered—on live TV—and then vanished; having the circumstances of your loved one's loss be the cause for 24-hour media attention; having world leaders and celebrities insert themselves into your tragedy; and having all kinds of opportunists seize the moment for their own interests are layers built onto your tragedy that few outside of those affected can relate to. It would have been easy to see Sally's public persona and pigeonhole her as just an angry 9/11 mother. Just as the nightmare Sally was living was not one-dimensional—the loss of her son was compounded with all the other facets of 9/11 named above—it would be wrong to consider her reaction to the attacks as one-dimensional. Yes, she fought for change and I think that fighting gave her a purpose to carry on in those dark days. But at the heart of the matter, she was a mother who lost her son. Neither I nor anyone else could change that. I couldn't take away her pain.

Regardless, the time had come to plan a memorial for Christian. But first I had to convince Sally there was no chance her son was alive.

**

It was late one night, maybe three weeks after the attacks, at Lillie's. Kevin Dillon and I were talking. We knew what needed to be done. Though no trace of their loved ones had yet to be found, we needed to tell the families in no uncertain terms that their husbands, fathers, and sons were dead. Kevin had become very close to the Rodriguez family. Anthony and his wife Evelyn had been expecting their sixth child on September 11 and the baby, a girl, was born September 14. Hospital staff called the baby Hope, but Evelyn wanted to wait until Anthony came home to officially name her.[39] When that never happened, she followed her husband's wishes and called her Morgan.[40] The new baby gave the family a whole other level of emotions and—in a practical sense—things to do. The Rodriguez family was also waiting to plan a memorial. Kevin and I knew we needed to talk to the families, but we wanted to be sure we were doing the right thing. Kevin took a big swig of his beer.

"How are you going to tell Sally?" he asked. He knew how hard she had pushed back at the media and politicians whenever any of them were ready to declare her son dead.

"I don't know," I answered, afraid to even think of the conversation to be had.

"Let's go," he said as he slammed the empty bottle down on the table. Kevin had about 16 years on the job. He was short and wiry—usually dirty from having just fixed something. He was one of the guys who always took charge to get things done around the firehouse. He worked fast. Everything he did was fast.

"Now?" I answered as I hurriedly finished my beer. I knew I was going with him and I wasn't about to waste it.

"Right now."

Kevin and I walked straight from the bar to the Battery Tunnel. We hitched a ride through, in the back of a pick-up as usual, and walked up to the site. We were in civilian clothes but were allowed through with our ID's. Kevin and I stood about 30 feet back from a huge, compacted, pile of twisted steel and debris. An excavating machine tugged away pieces and cops and firemen sifted through the wreckage. We stood there and watched. I had, of course, seen the work up close before. Plenty of times— while digging or manning a bucket brigade—I would take a moment to look around at the devastation and take in the enormity of the tragedy. But somehow this time was different. I had never stood back as a spectator. What were we looking for? I can't really say. I think we just needed to see one more time just how horrific the collapse was in order to face what we knew all along. They were really gone. I looked over to Kevin. He had tears running down his cheeks. He put his arm around me and we watched the excavator wave its unfeeling arm at the horror. After a while, we walked back to the tunnel.

The next day I would drive up to see the Regenhards.

**

I sat on the couch in Christina's apartment and nervously fumbled out the sentence I had been dreading.

I told Sally that I didn't believe there was any way Christian was still alive and that since there had been no trace of any of the guys from Engine 279, it would probably be good to plan a memorial service. I had worked myself up into such a frenzy over that announcement that I don't remember now the exact words I used—I just vaguely remember sitting on that couch and blurting it out. What I will never forget, however, is Sally's reaction. She told me that they had been thinking about going to Saint Patrick's Cathedral.

They had been thinking about it. There was no argument, no push back. She was ready to start planning. It was a sign of Sally's strength. Her public protests were not the rantings of a woman in denial. They were concrete actions taken to ensure no stone was left unturned. When it was time to fight, Sally fought. There would be more fights ahead, but for the moment it was time to say goodbye to Christian. Sally accepted this, apparently before I even had to tell her. That week, I went with Sally, Christina, and Al to Saint Patrick's to check availability and book a date in late October.

The memorial was a couple of weeks away and there was plenty to do in the meantime. Kevin had likewise set a date with the Rodriguez family and Gary Kakeh was in the process of making arrangements for Ronnie Henderson's memorial. Mike Ragusa's parents chose to wait. They were terrified of going through the ordeal of a memorial only to then be notified of Mike's remains being found and having to do it all again. As it turns out, Mike's memorial would be the last funeral or memorial the FDNY would hold, almost two years later in September of 2003.[§§] We decided to keep the same guys who had been

---

[§§]There would be burial ceremonies after that date in cases where remains were identified by DNA, but these were cases where the

in contact with the families as the coordinator for the memorials. It was about this time these individuals were given an official title—*family liaison.*

How did one become a family liaison? There was no one method. It was an unpaid position that came with no training or instruction. Some firehouses named one person as liaison for all families and took that individual off the work chart to deal exclusively with multiple families. This sometimes burned the liaison out and some firehouses rotated individuals into the position. Other firehouses chose to name one liaison per family. In Engine 279 and Ladder 131, our liaisons stayed on the chart, working our scheduled shifts, and performed our liaison duties largely on our own time, though we spent a lot of our on-duty time making liaison-related phone calls. The system worked well. The families developed a trusted rapport with the liaisons and having one individual remain with each family ensured a continuity of information between families and the firehouse. The liaisons themselves were then responsible to delegate responsibilities among other members of the firehouse. Quite often, I would ask one of the guys to track down some information or help make some arrangement and I could then move on to the next issue confident all would be taken care of. The Regenhard family, for example, may never even have known of the network of support from the guys at the firehouse—they just got the phone call from me saying it had been taken care of. The system made things easier for the families. One phone call from me was simpler than a dozen calls from guys doing different things.

---

individual already had a memorial service. This statement also excludes fire and EMS personnel who would subsequently die as a result of 9/11 related illnesses.

I never minded one bit being a family liaison. Sure there was a lot to do—but I wanted to do more. I hated the days when I felt I wasn't doing something to help the family. I was single at the time, no kids. I was able to devote myself to being a liaison without much strain on my family life. Kevin Dillon and Gerry Sweeney, however, were married with young kids. Every minute they spent looking after the families meant time away from their own families. To a certain extent, Gary Kakeh experienced this too, though his kids were older. We were working at the firehouse a lot. In the early weeks, we were at the site digging a lot. We were now attending funerals and memorials a lot. All firefighters were busy every day with the aftermath of the attacks; free time at home was almost nonexistent. Liaisons spent what free time they had looking after the families of the fallen. Only Kevin and Gerry could say exactly what it was like for them balancing their own family life and their liaison work.

A cell phone company loaned hundreds of mobile phones to the Fire Department for the families and liaisons to use. It was an early-model gray brick with a pull-up antenna, but it was free. Sally got one and so did I. The Fire Department now had a Family Assistance Unit up and running, as well as the Ceremonial Unit. Organization was returning to headquarters and an extended network fell into place. Because I had been using my personal cell phone up until that point, many of the contacts I had made were still using that number. So I needed both phones with me at all times.

I was in the firehouse kitchen once when both phones rang at the same time. As I took them both out of my pocket to decide which to answer, a cackle erupted around the table.

"What is this a fucking contest?" Chris Kielczewski quipped. "He who has the most cell phones wins!"

I was in constant contact with the Family Assistance Unit and the Ceremonial guys—relaying information back and forth with the Regenhards as Christian's memorial took shape. There were calls to and from the Cathedral staff, the police precinct, the bagpipe band, the restaurant for the luncheon after the memorial, and countless others. If there was any point after 9/11 when I strained under the stress, this was it. There was a two-week stretch when my phone rang so often I almost had a nervous breakdown. I couldn't relax—my mind was racing. If I wasn't on a call, I was convinced I was forgetting to return a call. If it was late at night and I wasn't on the phone with Sally, Christina, or Al, I felt guilty for it. The gray phone was always there—always reminding me that I was forgetting to do something. The feeling never went away. To this day, if a series of phone calls needs to be made or someone is waiting for me to call them back, I get anxious. I regress back to those weeks after 9/11 and I become overwhelmed. I find it hard to make any calls. It frustrates my wife that I'm so bad at making phone calls and I've never found a way to tell her why I'm so averse to it.

Until now.

I was glad when the cell phone company eventually asked for the phones back. My stress was of course dwarfed by the strain on the Regenhard family. Grief is the most private of emotions and funerals, in general, force you to share your grief with others. The pomp and ceremony of a Fire Department funeral mixed with the worldwide attention brought on by the 9/11 attacks made Christian's memorial a public event. Sally, Al, and Christina handled the stress as well as could be expected. While the situation was hard—dealing with them was never difficult. I had a job to do and in many ways, they got me through it. The genuine kindness they showed toward me propelled me forward.

**

Firefighters are commonly sent out of their firehouse to cover a shift elsewhere. Each company has a minimum staffing level to maintain and if a unit is shorthanded on any given tour, and a neighboring company has an extra firefighter reporting, he or she will be temporarily assigned, or "detailed" in Fire Department lingo, to the company in need. As a result, firefighters in the same battalion get to know each other fairly well and have a good sense for what is happening in the other houses. A few weeks after 9/11, I was detailed to Ladder 118, in Brooklyn Heights, to cover a day tour.

Eight members of Engine 205/Ladder 118 were killed in the World Trade Center attacks.*** There were eight families to take care of. When I reported for my detail in Ladder 118 that morning, I was immediately impressed by the system put in place to organize the effort. Two of the senior men, Ed Greene and Richie Murray, oversaw the operation. Each family was assigned a liaison who functioned much as the liaisons did in Engine 279/Ladder 131.[41] In the kitchen of their Middagh Street firehouse, an impromptu operations center was established. A ledger book was used to record and pass along all information regarding remains found, memorial and funeral plans, families' needs, and any other issue arising. While the liaisons dealt with the families on a

---

***Lieutenant Robert Regan, Firefighters Leon Smith, Vernon Cherry, Peter Vega, Scott Davidson, and Joseph Agnello of Ladder 118 were killed. Lieutenant Robert Wallace of Engine 205 was killed while working in Engine 226 and Captain Martin Egan, who had been a lieutenant in Ladder 118 and promoted just months before 9/11, was also killed while working in a covering assignment.

one-on-one basis, any member of the firehouse answering the phone was expected to record the transaction in the ledger and take swift action to resolve any issue needing immediate attention.[42] Retired members came in to help answer the phones and greet the never-ending throng of visitors.

Much like Engine 279/Ladder 131's experience with having a line-of-duty death a few years prior to 9/11 to draw from, Ladder 118 had lost Firefighter Phillip D'Adamo in 1984 and the senior members had a good idea from the outset of what needed to be done, even if the scale had now grown eightfold. "Being a liaison wasn't new," said Firefighter Richie Murray.[43] "They just gave it a name." The liaisons from Engine 205/Ladder 118 kept in constant contact with the families of the fallen men as the months dragged on. All of the members of the firehouse balanced working their regular shifts, going to the Trade Center site to search for remains, going to memorials and funerals, and caring for the families. Widows and parents needed help with everything from paperwork to house and auto repairs; children needed everything from Santa to sports coach. The senior men of 205 and 118 also knew it was important that the surviving firefighters take care of each other as well. "I told the guys to always be patient, and keep it up," remembered Murray.[44] "While you're in mourning, [having things to do] is a good thing," he explained. "I would have lost my mind had I not been busy—at the end of the day exhausted."[45]

On New Year's Eve, the bodies of Lieutenant Robert Regan, and Firefighters Joe Agnello, Vernon Cherry, and Peter Vega were found, starting a succession of funerals for the liaisons to coordinate. The burden was well distributed with all members of the firehouse doing their part, but the job of writing eulogies—all eight eulogies—

went to Firefighter John Sorrentino.[46] I know how hard it is to find a way to sum up everything that was special about a brother firefighter and I know how difficult it can be to organize your thoughts into something coherent, let alone moving. Sorrentino was the right man for the job and I don't know whether his Herculean effort impresses me more as a fireman or as a writer.

While I was assigned to Ladder 131, I worked quite a few details in Engine 205/Ladder 118, both before and after 9/11. The small kitchen, crammed in a room behind the two side-by-side rigs was always the heart of the firehouse. Larger-than-life characters like Vernon Cherry and Leon Smith held court and I remember sitting in the corner laughing so hard my side hurt. The surviving members continued the same tradition—the kitchen was the support network. Engine 205/Ladder 118 took a huge hit on 9/11. The loss was devastating, but their response was inspiring. I'm sure the members themselves, and certainly the liaisons, had many trying moments, but from the outside looking in, they seemed extremely well organized. The aftermath of Phillip D'Adamo's death, perhaps, taught them to rely on each other, and even counseling, early on.[47]

**

Other liaisons didn't fare so well. At some point—maybe late October or early November—the Fire Department's Counseling Unit offered a therapy session for family liaisons. Kevin asked me to go with him. The meeting was held at the Unit's Lafayette Street facility on the top floor of Ladder 20's firehouse. Only a dozen or so of the hundreds of liaisons showed up. Firemen aren't known for talking about their feelings. The stories those guys told were heartbreaking. Some were liaisons for the families of guys who had been their best friends, some were handling multiple families, and the most common theme—the issue a majority of the guys were struggling with the most—was the strain on their family life. One guy broke down and cried as he described his own wife threatening divorce if he didn't spend more time at home with his kids while he found himself wracked with guilt anytime he wasn't with his fallen buddy's kids. Some described their own wives as intensely jealous they were spending so much time with the widows. I felt horrible for all of them. I didn't speak during the meeting. I had nothing to complain about.

The session was intense. Afterward, Kevin and I needed a drink. I suggested McSorley's. I had always loved McSorley's nineteenth-century charm and I was in the mood for some part of my old life. It was a weeknight—not very crowded. A handful of college students and tourists were spread around the saw-dusted floor-space at small tables. Kevin and I stood at the bar. I don't remember what we talked about that night—only one detail stands out in my memory. At some point, a guy at the bar, who was about my age, turned to the side and sprinkled cocaine on his fingernail. He slyly put it to his nose and snorted. It was quick and stealth and I was probably the only one who noticed.

McSorley's isn't exactly a hotbed of drug activity; I had never seen anything like that there before. But he was completely at ease and went right on having a good time with his group of friends. They laughed. Life was normal. They were my age and seemed to have no clue what was going on a couple of miles south at the Trade Center.

**

Engine 54, Ladder 4, and Battalion 9 lost 15 members on 9/11. The strain of caring for 15 families (with dozens of children) must have been enormous. Lieutenant Bob Jackson of Engine 54 took a leading role with organizing all of the funerals and memorials,[48] an astounding feat considering the emotional toll planning one memorial took on me. Jackson summed up the firehouse's response in a 2002 interview: "We circled the wagons for the widows... And we still do."[49] The sheer number of families meant the liaison work needed to be divided and duties rotated but the surviving members of the firehouse were dedicated to the long-term well being of the families. "We keep in contact with them all the time, these 15 families. They know that whatever they need, whenever they need it, they can call here and we're going to take care of them,"[50] Firefighter Joe Ceravolo of Ladder 4 told a reporter, *12 years* after 9/11. "They're not going to be forgotten—ever,"[51] he reiterated. I can only imagine how it felt to live through the months after 9/11 in the firehouse—just like we did in Engine 279/Ladder 131 and they did in Engine 205/Ladder118 and maybe even to a more heightened degree with 15 men killed—only to be hit with the additional burden of having to defend the men you lost against allegations that they weren't heroes at all, but petty criminals. Battalion Chief Joseph Nardone of Battalion 9 described his reaction to reading about the allegations:

> My wife was not with me at the time. When she pulled up, she said, 'What's wrong?' I said, 'I just read something that's just incredibly unbelievable to me.' I'm here to say that I knew that entire crew for over 11 years. There was no finer crew in the New York City Fire Department working that day. Every one of those men were professional, dedicated and were out for one thing: to save people.[52]

Certainty of the men's innocence did not soften the blow. Now, on top of all the things firehouses across the city were dealing with: working in the firehouse, training new members, rotations down at the Trade Center site, attending countless funerals, planning their own memorials and funerals, and caring for the families of the men lost; the members of Engine 54, Ladder 4, and Battalion 9 had another enormous weight dropped on them. They would have to fight to clear their brothers' names.

I speak as someone who lived through that time in a firehouse and can only imagine what it was like in their firehouse. I can't even begin to imagine what news of these allegations did to the families of the men who died.

CHAPTER 7

ON FRIDAY, OCTOBER 26, 2001, a memorial service was held at Saint Patrick's Cathedral for Firefighter Christian Regenhard. Word had indeed spread across the country that the FDNY needed help with funeral attendance. Men and women in uniform arrived in waves—the LA firefighters in the yellow school bus had been just the tip of the iceberg. They came from big cities and small towns—professional firefighters and volunteers. The fact that Christian's service was six weeks after the attacks (time enough for the call for mourners to get out and for travel arrangements to be made) and the location of the memorial—Midtown Manhattan—combined to make this particular memorial one of the largest attended services of all. The procession went south of the cathedral for blocks and blocks—over ten thousand uniformed men and women lined Fifth Avenue.

A couple of weeks before, I had been told by the Fire Department's Emerald Society Pipes and Drums Band that they could not guarantee bagpipers for Christian's service and that we should have a backup plan. One of the guys in the firehouse knew some bagpipers from his town and we had a handful of them ready to march. In the end, they weren't necessary as the Fire Department bagpipers showed up in force at Saint Pat's. I'm sure that two weeks out it was hard for them to predict how thin they would be spread, but God bless those guys, I never attended a memorial or funeral where the Pipes and

Drums guys didn't make a strong showing, even if it was just a handful of them due to multiple simultaneous funerary commitments. It could not have been easy for them but they never quit. They seemed to be everywhere and, what's more, they themselves worked in firehouses that lost guys. They went down to the site and dug. They took care of the families of the fallen. And, they beat the drum; they blew the pipes. They marched the brothers home.

I was nervous as hell. The church would be packed—3,000 people were expected to fill the pews—and I was to give a eulogy. The members of Engine 279 and Ladder 131 stood ready, north of the cathedral, while the final preparations were made. The ceremonial fire truck was idling, the bagpipers tuned their instruments, and I paced around trying to work out the jitters. Gerry Sweeney came over to me and patted me on the back.

"You doing OK?" he asked bluntly. Gerry always sounded like a football coach at halftime.

I nodded.

He put his arm around me and leaned into my ear. "You're doing a great job. It's gonna be fine."

Gerry was never shy about telling somebody they were fucking up. If he said I was doing a great job, it meant something. I took a deep breath and relaxed. "Let's do this," I said.

Gerry nodded. He was one of the rocks of the firehouse. Every firehouse had one—or more. I was lucky to have Gerry. There may not have been a playbook to follow on how to be a liaison, but I never had to wonder what the right thing looked like. Gerry was the model.

We lined up behind the rig and marched in step to the Cathedral's stairs. The drums rattled a perfect cadence and the bagpipes echoed off the tall buildings. When *Amazing Grace* had finished, Sally, Christina, and Al led a procession of family, friends, politicians and dignitaries, members of Engine 279 and Ladder 131, and almost 3,000 others up the aisle of the Saint Patrick's massive nave. The mayor spoke. While controversy would later surface surrounding Rudy Giuliani's actions after 9/11 as politics would come to overshadow much of the tragedy; I don't think anyone would disagree that the mayor did an exceptional job speaking at funerals and memorials. He was eloquent, reflective, comforting, and uplifting. Commissioner Von Essen and Cardinal Egan also spoke. Sally showed great poise in giving a moving summary of her son's life. Then it was my turn.

I told the congregation that Christian's nickname at the firehouse was Braveheart (a play off the movie title and his name—Regenhard). I spoke about how fitting the name was for the film's title character's description of the Scottish army—*Warrior Poets.* Christian embodied this description. He was a highly trained Marine sergeant who wrote thoughtful vignettes in his journals, a rock climber and an impressionist painter. I told the audience about how Christian seemed shy at first, but in the days after September 11, at least three young women introduced themselves to me as Christian's girlfriend. I told of how Christian helped rescue an unconscious man from an apartment fire and performed CPR, though the man would unfortunately die of his injuries. Christian made his mark on the world. That is what I tried to convey.

I stepped back from the podium and toward Sally, Christina, and Al in the front pew. A deacon tugged at my arm and nodded his head toward the seated cardinal. I think I was supposed to bow toward His Eminence or something. I went straight to Sally and hugged her, then Christina, and Al gave me a hearty handshake. The day was for them, not the dignitaries.

All uniformed personnel lined up outside. The family exited the cathedral and stopped on the sidewalk adjacent the ceremonial fire truck. I did my best to make the Marine in Al proud as I marched forward holding a fire helmet emblazoned with a red and white 131 and Christian's badge number beneath (the helmet was new as Christian's was never found). Searching, somehow, for both stern dignity and loving warmth, I spoke:

On behalf of the Fire Department of the City of New York and a grateful city, please accept this helmet as a symbol of our appreciation for your loved one's honorable and faithful service.

Once my words were done I handed the helmet to Sally. I took one step backward while keeping my body straight toward the front. I snapped off the smartest military salute I could muster, held for a second, and then brought my arm down cleanly parallel to my trouser seam. I took another step back, turned and marched to my place in the company formation. I'm sure it wasn't Marine Corps quality, but I did my best to carry out the tradition.

**

After Ronnie, Anthony, and Christian's memorials, a certain—however strange—calm settled down over the firehouse. By mid-November, we really weren't going down to the site to dig on our own time anymore. The Department had implemented the 30-day rotation system and each firehouse sent one or two guys at a time. I was still a family liaison so Captain Ford didn't put me in the rotation. I worked my regular tours at the firehouse. We still went to funerals and memorials regularly. The guys from Ladder 131 who had survived the collapse: Lieutenant Gary Wood, Keith Kaiser, Mark Ruppert, Troy Owens, and Matty Castrogiovanni had returned to work. Craig Gutkes, who had been the company chauffeur on September 11, however, did not. Craig was injured in the collapse and was for a time separated from the other members of Ladder 131. He searched and called on the radio, trying desperately to locate the other members of his company. He had miraculously survived a skyscraper practically falling on top of him and his first thought was the safety of others. His injuries, however, prevented him from returning to duty.

It was around this time that Lieutenant Coleman called me into the office. The Department had put out a request for any member who might be interested in transferring to the Special Operations Command. SOC, as the command is known consists of rescue and squad companies, highly trained technical rescue units, and hazardous material teams. I had expressed my interest to Lieutenant Coleman before, after one of the days on the pile when SOC guys had been crawling into voids and rappelling into craters while the rest of us were on bucket brigades. He helped me with the application and the following day, Captain Ford called the captain of Squad 1, a friend of his, and gave me a good recommendation.

I was accepted and told to report to Rescue School in January. The specialized training in SOC would normally have taken place over a couple of years for new members. The heavy losses endured by SOC units on September 11, however, necessitated an abbreviated initiation course— three weeks. I left Ladder 131 with a heavy heart. I had gone through a terrible time with those guys, and I loved them. My time at the Trade Center, however, convinced me that I needed to be at the center of the action. I saw what those guys did to save John McLoughlin and I wanted to be one of them. It was a strange time in America and especially New York. We were all convinced more attacks were coming. I wanted to be as ready as possible for the next one.

**

It was strange to hang my gear on the rack in a spot that belonged to a guy that died. Squad 1 lost eleven men on September 11 plus a former member who had spent 20 years in the company, just recently been promoted to lieutenant, and died working in another company. The squad was in a firehouse by themselves (not a double house like Engine 279 and Ladder 131), so there were fewer firefighters assigned. The remaining men were dealing with 12 families, planning twelve funerals (or memorials), and training the eleven new members that would be needed to fill the roster. After three weeks at the Rescue School, I started work at Squad 1 in late January 2002. In addition to the firefighters assigned to the Trade Center on 30-day rotations, the Department decided that there would always be a SOC unit present at the site. There were seven squads and five rescue companies and each company was assigned on a rotating basis. One company was sent from 9 AM to 6 PM, another company was sent from 6 PM to midnight, and a third company was sent from midnight to 9 AM. So every third or fourth day, Squad 1 spent a shift at the site.

On average, I went once or twice a week. I had not been there since the night Kevin and I walked over from the bar. It was different. Most work now was below grade. There were no more bucket brigades. The material was pulled apart by large excavating machines and then sifted by small teams of cops and firefighters. Officially, the SOC units were assigned as a rapid intervention team, should a recovery worker become trapped or injured. We drove to the site with our rig and all of our rescue gear, but once there we usually took turns. Three of us would wait by the rig with the rescue gear, while three of us donned Carhartt overalls and helped with the digging. It was on a midnight to 9 AM shift mid-March that Rob Maddalone and I found John Tipping.

CHAPTER 8

LIFE WOULD NEVER GO BACK to the way it was before September 11, but a new normal did slowly take over. I was still very close with the Regenhard family. There would be much work ahead for Sally in her advocacy role leading the Skyscraper Safety Campaign, fighting for improved fire safety and building codes, as well as being a leading voice for the 9/11 Parents and Families. Many players would vie for power in the decisions to be made over the fate of the Trade Center site and the planned memorial. Sally and others fought to ensure the families' voices were heard. I attended meetings and rallies with her when I could. I also went back to college.

I passed the exam for promotion to lieutenant and was given a list number that figured to have me promoted in two years or so. I attended more specialized training courses at the Rescue School and settled in to the new reality. Work was challenging. The Special Operations Command was everything I thought it would be. We responded to all sorts of emergencies: collapses, auto extrications, rope rescues, hazardous materials spills, and all serious fires in western and southern Brooklyn as well as all of Staten Island. It was highly engaging and the perfect outlet for me to pour myself into my professional life. There was still the occasional funeral or memorial to attend and Squad 1—with twelve lost members' families to consider—was still dealing heavily with the emotional stresses that I had experienced in the first months after the attacks in Engine 279/Ladder 131. Some time that summer the Fire Department contracted the help of dozens of psychologists to start making regular visits to any firehouse which lost members.

We at Squad 1 had Doctor Bob, or so we called him. He was a genuinely caring therapist who came by the firehouse once a week for dinner. He got to know all of the members and patiently observed the issues facing the firehouse. He listened always and offered advice when appropriate. Even the guys who had been against letting a "stranger" into our business came to like Doctor Bob. The lingering effects of such a massive loss and the struggles to put the company back together were challenges that showed effects in a wide array of seemingly unrelated issues around the firehouse and Doctor Bob's observations were therapeutic.

I don't remember ever really opening up to Doctor Bob. This period (summer/fall 2002), however, was about the time I first heard about William Langewiesche's allegations. I remember watching a news story on TV in Squad 1's kitchen. The reporter said that the author claimed a group of firefighters had been looting the Gap prior to the collapse. I watched with disgust. As the recovery effort at the site had been closed in May and the summer months crept in, the media's fascination with "heroic" firemen had been showing signs of cracking. Firefighters arrested for bar fights or driving drunk went from being blurbs in the daily police blotter to front-page headlines. The looting story struck me as just a continuation of the trend. Firefighters were being knocked off their pedestal. The story ended by naming another company—not Ladder 4—as the company in question while showing stock footage of a ladder apparatus.

It pissed me off, for sure. No company would have blown off helping people for free jeans. But it wasn't until the next time I came across the story that I felt the full weight of anger and betrayal. This time the reporter did not mix up the company. Though unnamed in Langewiesche's account, the details such as the location of the rig—five stories below grade—left no doubt. He was writing about Ladder 4.[†††] I heard Ladder 4 and thought about John Tipping. I was instantly back on the pile, kneeling and cradling his remains with my trembling hands. I thought of the look on his father's face when he arrived to carry his boy out of the pit. *What will his family think? How could anyone write such a thing?* I didn't know a single detail but I knew the story was false. I was many things after September 11: Heartbroken—yes; anxious for the future—at times; angry—sure, but only in vague terms, meaning angry at the terrorists though I didn't know any and had no recourse. But now a new type of rage took over.

9/11 was difficult in myriad ways. The one feeling that got me through it was pride. I don't feel anything that I did was particularly heroic, but I have always been proud to serve in the same department with so many truly noble people. The firemen who died had sacrificed themselves nobly in a desperate attempt to save lives. I felt that, at the very least, future generations would praise their sacrifice. But now I wasn't sure. William Langewiesche was a famous author and his book was

---

[†††]Langewiesche refers to the company as "this particular crew" (p. 161) and does not specifically name them as Ladder 4, a fact he has repeatedly touted as proof he is innocent of besmirching 4 Truck (see *NPR* interview and afterword to 2011 paperback edition listed in endnotes). Ladder 4's being the only rig to be smashed down into the shopping concourse, the company was widely reported to be the crew in question from the outset.

getting a lot of attention. His story would surely become part of the *history* of 9/11. History would remember that firemen who showed up at the World Trade Center had their own selfish agenda. It didn't matter that not everyone would believe it. Some people would believe it and it angered me to my core.

I don't remember when I first had the dream, but I know it was this very anger that brought it on. *It's dark and stormy. I stand on the bank of a fast moving river, knee deep in water. Flowing past me, by the hundreds, are firemen. Their unmistakable helmets bob in the white spraying current and they wave their arms toward me as they go by. I reach out to grab one—then another. But they're moving too quickly and the current is too strong. Dozens slip through my hands. I can't save them. I watch in horror as many slip under the waves and don't return. Behind me is a fire chief. He is safely on dry land and looking on helplessly. "I told you!" I yell at the chief. "I told you!"* I wake in my bed, tossing and turning, muttering "I told you" over and over.

I won't speculate on the deeper meaning of my dream. I just know that whenever I woke from it, I would lay awake the rest of the night—seething. I don't know how many times it happened. The dream—and the underlying anger—was a part of my new reality. It was a reality that I can reflect upon now as being out of proportion to the triggering event. A journalist had written a book—albeit a flawed one with which I have many disagreements—but it was just a book. There were far worse crimes. After all, terrorists had just murdered three thousand people. I had run a full gamut of emotions after the attacks, but overall I think I coped well. Now a book unhinged me.

Imagine a man driving home from work. He gets a flat tire and remembers there is no spare in the trunk. He does not worry because he is an AAA member. He calls to find out his membership has lapsed, and worse, he left his wallet at home. Again, he handles the news well and decides to walk. Halfway home it begins to rain. He does not complain while his clothes become soaked. At his front door, he remembers that he left his house keys back in the car. He does not despair and is able to climb up a tree into a second floor window, despite falling once and skinning his knee while becoming covered in mud. He finally gets inside, takes off his wet clothes, and slips on a bathrobe. All he wants is a hot cup of tea. He puts a pot to boil and goes in the cupboard for a teabag. The box is empty. The man becomes enraged and throws the box on the floor, stomping on it repeatedly while cursing at the top of his lungs.

Looking back, you could say the man overreacted to having run out of teabags. But in the overall context of the bad day he was having, one could see his outburst as the release point of a lot of pent up anger. For me, William Langewiesche's allegations against Ladder 4 was that release point. Losing so many friends, seeing dead bodies and picking up body parts, telling a mother her son wasn't coming home were a succession of experiences that led to me now wanting to stomp on a copy of *American Ground* while cursing at the top of my lungs.

My experiences pale in comparison to countless others who went through far worse, but I still feel justified in my anger. After all, we're not talking about teabags. We're talking about the legacy of seven men who gave their lives. It would be many years before I could see my anger as the culmination of all my 9/11 experiences. In 2002, however, my rage had one font—the "liar" William Langewiesche.

**

I spent the next few years stuck in the same pattern. Life moved on, of course. I finally earned a bachelor's degree and I got promoted to lieutenant. My personal life was a series of rather short relationships. Sometimes I broke it off; sometimes they left me. Even though the girls I dated were perfectly lovely people, I was restless. I didn't know what I was looking for; I just knew I hadn't found it. Every so often the dream would come back and the anger—always just below the surface—would return. Few around me probably ever sensed the rage I walked around with. I hid it well. I enjoyed a cold beer, don't get me wrong, but I didn't fall into substance abuse. I didn't snap at friends and family. Outwardly I was fine. At night, however, I often lay awake stewing. It's not like I thought 9/11 would ever sit well with me. It's not the type of experience one makes peace with. But somehow just knowing Langewiesche's story was out there made it harder to live with. *American Ground* repudiated the selfless bravery of my brothers, so it invalidated many of the things I was most proud of. I went on like this until mid-2007, I think.

Then, one night, I was sunk deep into the couch cushions with my legs crossed on the long sectional before me. I balanced an almost empty bottle of beer on my lap and flipped through channels lazily without even lifting the remote control off the couch. Images zoomed by as I pressed the button repeatedly. I paused at footage of a World Trade Center tower collapsing. It was brief and cut to another video of the streets of Pompeii. The title of the show was flashed across the screen— *American Vesuvius*—and the announcer said something about how events on 9/11 were similar to Mt. Vesuvius's eruption. Before he finished his sentence I had changed the channel—my lazy relaxation now spoiled with cynical indignation. *They'll do anything for ratings,* I thought. *What does Pompeii have to do with 9/11?*

I took another sip of beer and tried to find something else to watch. My mind raced for a few minutes—the collapsing tower playing over and over again. Before I knew it I had gone through all of the channels and was now on my second loop.

"And his methods have been used to vindicate a crew of firefighters," said the narrator's voice before I realized I had returned to *American Vesuvius.* An image of an FDNY ladder truck was on the screen. I set the bottle down on the coffee table and sat up pointing the remote at the TV furiously. *Volume damn it!*

Charles Pellegrino, read the subtext while a studious yet casual looking middle-aged man spoke about a group of firefighters accused of stealing. He described how, while researching his book *Ghosts of Vesuvius,* he noticed similarities between the damage done by the collapsing pyroclastic column of Mount Vesuvius's eruption and the collapsing towers of the World Trade Center. He explains what he calls "shock cocoons," where the energy of the collapsing column is directed around certain objects, leaving them unscathed.[53] Likewise, a fire truck could have been crushed and destroyed by a collapsing tower while merchandise from a clothing store could have survived in their boxes unscathed.

At the next commercial break I ran to my computer and searched for *Ghosts of Vesuvius* on Amazon. I received the order confirmation email before the break was over.

**

I devoured *Ghosts of Vesuvius.* The breakdown of Pompeii's demise, filled with Roman history and scientific curiosities fascinated me. Pellegrino goes on to seamlessly parallel so called shock cocoons found in excavations at Pompeii, Herculaneum and the wreckage of the World Trade Center. Of particular interest, was how different rooms of some houses near Vesuvius experienced wildly differing degrees of damage: one room could be completely incinerated while the next room over could be perfectly preserved, with food set out on the table in some instances.[54] When I finally arrived at his findings of Ladder 4's ordeal, I had butterflies in my stomach and my hands trembled exactly as they had when I held John Tipping's remains. Pellegrino coolly describes the contradictory forces that left annihilation and preservation side by side. My eyes watered reading him describe "how 4 Truck, as it was hammered five stories below street level with a force approaching three tons per square inch... passed hundreds of *unbroken* wine bottles."[55]

Pellegrino's description of a wine cellar in the concourse level mostly surviving the collapse is a perfect example of his "shock cocoon" theory. [56] He then summarizes the incredulity that often accompanies such phenomena:

> Still... none of this knowledge could discourage the publication of public indictments against the crew of Ladder 4, entirely on the basis of folded jeans from a clothing warehouse coming to rest in orderly piles, near (but in fact not on or in) 4 Truck. At first glance, it had seemed impossible, to some, that order could arise within such chaos without the intervention of human hands. If the work of gravity currents was an inkblot test, in which one sees what one wants to see, there were certainly those who (perhaps acting out of rage against the ruins themselves) saw something more sinister at work in nature's physics.[57]

The first thought that went through my head was history's judgment. Perhaps now—finally—there would be some rebuttal to *American Ground.* Perhaps there was some chance that Ladder 4 would not be cursed by posterity. There would be some explanation for what had appeared so hard to explain—almost impossible to explain. "It was hard," adds Pellegrino, "so a writer claimed and so his editor upheld, to avoid the conclusion that Ladder 4 was at the center of 'a widespread pattern of looting that started even before the Towers fell.'"[58]

Pellegrino would go on to dismantle that conclusion. Unlike so many who perished that Tuesday morning, the crew of Ladder 4 had many witnesses to their final moments. He cites witnesses like Captain Paul Mallery who was treating injured evacuees gathered inside Engine 10/Ladder 10 (across the street from the World Trade Center) and watched Ladder 4 park in front of the South Tower. Mallery describes how the men of 4 Truck dodged falling debris and jumpers to get to the lobby.[59] Pellegrino describes how Linda Rothemund squeezed through a narrow opening in a jammed elevator door and brought the firefighters to the elevator to rescue the other trapped occupants—who were being burned by flaming jet fuel dripping from above. He describes how a woman named Lauren Smith was saved by Ladder 4.[60]

Pellegrino also tells the story of Firefighter Tim Brown, who was assigned to the Office of Emergency Management and was in the South Tower lobby and witnessed Ladder 4's actions. [61] Finally, Pellegrino describes how FEMA cameraman Patrick Drury videotaped the excavation of 4 Truck and would later report that no jeans, folded or otherwise, were found inside Ladder 4's rig.[62]

The first thing I did after finishing *Ghosts of Vesuvius* was go online and look up Charles Pellegrino. There was no contact information on his website, but it did list a street address for his literary agent. I penned a very emotional letter thanking him for his research and praising his book. I even added that I was in grad school—therefore used to research work—and interested in working on a book or article solely about Ladder 4's ordeal. *Ghosts of Vesuvius* was, after all, about much more and I didn't want 4 Truck's story getting overlooked. Deep down, I was hoping he would be tempted to write such a work himself. There was so much about this story I wanted to share but I didn't feel I could write it myself. I had such strong feelings about the issue that I didn't think I could possibly organize my thoughts. I didn't know where to even begin. It would take me ten more years to get over that. And Pellegrino was, after all, a *New York Times* Bestseller. The more *he* put the story out there, the more it would catch on. I mailed the letter to his agent. Pellegrino wrote me back.

He was very gracious and reiterated his own strong feelings about vindicating Ladder 4.‡‡‡ He told me of his plans to travel to Hiroshima and Nagasaki for research, vaguely described a possible future book about the World Trade Center, and invited me to join the discussion forum on his website. Pellegrino concluded by offering me help with the article I had told him I wanted to write. He did not, however, offer to write it for me. *Damn, he didn't take the bait.*

---

‡‡‡ We corresponded again two years later. In this later letter, Pellegrino claimed to be the victim of a severe backlash from the publishing industry over his rebuttal of Langewiesche's work.

CHAPTER 9

FEW PLACES ON EARTH combine natural beauty and violent history as artfully as Italy. The medieval cities of Tuscany are a living museum featuring centuries of intrigue and warfare behind picturesque ancient walls in the shadows of high lookout towers. I fell in love with the country's beauty and history while studying Italian literature at Hunter College. I had decided to learn Italian and took a handful of language courses. The more I learned the more I wanted to know. I was motivated to speak the language fluently by a combination of forces. I had vacationed in Italy in 2007 and enjoyed piecing together the tidbits of Italian I remembered from my childhood and from college courses years earlier. Then, as I started my journey toward conquering *la bella lingua,* I met Teresa.

The woman who would become my wife spent a large part of her childhood in Italy. She returned often to visit family and explore the country's culture and scenery. Her first language was Italian and I wanted very much to be able to travel around the Italian countryside with her experiencing *la dolce vita.* I completed the introductory language courses at Hunter and then enrolled in the advanced Italian literature program. I was captivated by the epic poets Dante, Petrarca, and Ariosto.

The spring of 2009 was unusually hot in Italy, but the weather throughout the country was clear in late May. I traveled to Italy that year for my wedding and honeymoon. It was Teresa's dream to be married in her family's native country and our family and friends were eager for an excuse to eat and drink their way across Tuscany. I enjoyed the trip very much. In Teresa, I had finally found what I had been searching for. The restlessness disappeared. What remained, however, was the anger—though it was less acute. In my mind, Pellegrino's work had acquitted Ladder 4 once and for all. Perhaps his book wasn't as famous as *American Ground,* but at least the facts were out there. I thought about John Tipping during my trip. I thought about him a lot. I was falling in love and getting married. I was traveling to amazing, far off places. I was living life—the life that was stolen from Tipping. I couldn't get the image of holding his remains out of my head. I thought about all he missed and about what Langewiesche had done to him. The anger was there with me.

One day on a train outside of Florence, I was thinking about the morning we found Tipping as I stared out the window. Just before, I had been practicing Italian phrases in my mind and a line rattled off my tongue:

Penso al retaggio di bugie che lui abbia,
e mi sveglio scuotendo con paura e rabbia.

I was describing the dream that wouldn't go away—the helplessness I felt. I couldn't help those drowning firemen. Whenever I thought of it, I would have a vision the second I awoke. I was back on the pile—holding Tipping.

I think of the legacy of lies that he has,
and I wake up shaking with fear and rage.

I repeated the lines over and over again—intrigued by the sing-song rhyme *abbia* and *rabbia.* I forgave myself the loose adherence to Italian's dreaded rules of the subjunctive case (*abbia,* have) and built outwards. Soon, I was writing a Renaissance-style epic poem in my little black Moleskine notepad. I spent the rest of my trip writing that poem—fifteen stanzas in all. I told of the night I first found Tipping and of seeing his dad come to carry the stretcher. I then introduced the poem's villain, the unnamed *giornalista* who peddled lies to sell books. *Sciacallo* is how I refer to him, which roughly translates to English's derogatory use of the word vulture. I go on to describe Ladder 4's true actions on 9/11 and the injustice of their false legacy. And then I wake up shaking—with fear and rage.

La battaglia per le anime nostre, I called it—*The Battle for Our Souls.* When I returned home in New York, I set to work translating the poem into English, which is harder than it sounds. Of course, my first language is English so it stands to reason that it should be simple to turn Italian phrases into English ones. But finding the right words in English to express the same exact thoughts while keeping the basic rhyme scheme and rhythm of the Italian took work. I didn't mind, however. It gave my mind a focus. I was still convinced that I needed to write about my experience at the Trade Center and about the injustice committed against the legacy of Ladder 4, but the thought of sitting down to type out a book frightened me. I didn't think I could ever focus my many deeply held feelings about 9/11 into a coherent story. A poem, on the other hand, was doable. Hell, I'd already done it. Now I just needed the world to hear it.

Simple, right?

If my poem gathered recognition, then Ladder 4's story would gather recognition and John Tipping would be acquitted, I reasoned. I decided to start where all social movements started—in a dark basement in Greenwich Village. There was an open mic poetry reading held at a popular bar and I signed up. I patiently sipped my beer with a rolled-up copy of *The Battle for Our Souls* in hand. One after another, poets young and old stood behind the microphone and poured out their feelings. Some were good and others, not. The host was very clear that the time limit was three minutes. I worried because in practice runs at home, the fastest I could read coherently brought my poem in about twenty seconds over. It seemed like some leeway was given if the audience liked the poet, but still I worried. The bistro tables jammed around the cozy cellar were packed with eager listeners and I wondered how my poem would be received. Some poets talked about personal hardships of one kind or another, but none broached anything as serious as 9/11. *What will they think?*

Finally, the host introduced me and I weaved through the tables and up on the stage. I said 'good evening' and with a nod to the host (who had her own microphone on the other side of the room) said "forgive me if I need an extra twenty seconds."

"Make it quick," the host rebutted without humor.

I cleared the lump in my throat and began.

On mountains of steel and hallowed dead...

I read in as smooth and even a tone as I could. I glanced up as I finished the first stanza, most in the room were still with me. On I went. With each stanza, more and more listeners broke away to whispered conversations among their tiny tables. I forged ahead hoping the last few lines would pack enough power to bring them back. But as I began the last line: *I wake up...* The host broke in and announced, "Time's up."

Had she been listening, she would have known that I was just about to finish. The rhyme scheme led to an inevitable *finale*. But she hadn't been listening. She was shuffling through papers on a table in the back and yelled, "Time's up," at the three-minute mark. It didn't seem like many in the audience had been listening either. The same people I had seen applaud wildly at a haiku about tree roots now gave a muted golf-clap. I looked around. One person applauded cheerfully. Her face glowed with pride and her eyes held my gaze firm. It was Teresa.

I learned a few things that night. First, poems are like political opinions—just because there are some good ones out there, doesn't mean anyone wants to hear yours. Second, I'm the luckiest guy in the world to have found a wife who loves and supports me in every way. And third, if the story of John Tipping and Ladder 4 was going to come from me, I was going to have to find some other medium.

Maybe I wasn't the right person to tell 4 Truck's story. At least Charles Pellegrino got the facts out there. If future generations wanted to learn the truth, they would have Pellegrino's undisputed findings to contend with. I was comforted by that even if I still held on to the anger. A few years later, however, I would learn that nothing is ever really undisputed.

**

The idea of writing a book about Ladder 4 never really left me. I just needed a spark—something to convince me that I could. While goofing around on the Internet one day, I found my spark. I typed in some search words about Ladder 4 and 9/11—on the lookout for some new breakthrough—and a story about Charles Pellegrino came up. I clicked on the link and then found another link. I read the disturbing news. In 2010, Pellegrino published *The Last Train from Hiroshima,* an investigative history of the atomic bombing of Japan during World War II. Soon after its release, the publisher was forced to pull the book due to the discovery that one of Pellegrino's sources had been a fraud. The publisher then found other problems with some of the witnesses interviewed and decided to stop printing the book altogether.[63]

For his part, Pellegrino admitted to being duped by the main witness (a man claiming to be a retired air force officer) but stood by his other sources.[64] It is beyond the scope of this book to delve into the veracity of Pellegrino's claims. What's relevant is that, rightly or wrongly, Pellegrino's reputation as a writer took a serious hit. I felt like I'd been kicked in the gut. *Would people now question* Ghosts of Vesuvius? That was the moment I knew I could write this book. I needed to write this book. I spent the next six months tracking down as many of the witnesses cited by Pellegrino as possible. Their stories needed to be presented without a cloud of suspicion over the presenter.

In the following chapter I will present as many witnesses as I could find to Ladder 4's actions on 9/11. Instances where I personally interviewed the witness will be noted, otherwise I have cited their stories from other sources (not *Ghosts of Vesuvius*). I will also present other evidence in support of my belief that not only did Ladder 4 *not* steal any merchandise on September 11; they died while directly engaged in rescuing trapped occupants of an elevator in the South Tower lobby.

Chapter 10

Located in Midtown, Ladder 4 was not initially assigned to the World Trade Center on the morning of September 11, 2001. [65] The incoming dayshift was scheduled to report to headquarters for annual medical exams and the company was to be unmanned that day. The first tower was struck at 8:46 in the morning. With such a tragedy unfolding and the night shift scheduled to end at 9:00, the crew of Ladder 4 made the decision to stay and staff the company even after their shift ended.[66] They were all technically off duty when dispatched downtown after the second tower was struck. They didn't have to go.

At approximately 9:09, seven minutes after the South Tower was struck, Ladder 4 can be heard responding. Lieutenant Dan O'Callaghan exhibits the hard charging spirit he was known for on the FDNY's Manhattan dispatcher recordings from September 11. Also heard on the recording is Lieutenant Gary Wood, from my company, Ladder 131:

O'Callaghan: "Four Truck to Manhattan. K."
Dispatcher: "Four Truck, Go ahead."
Wood: "Ladder One-Three-One to Manhattan."
Dispatcher: "Ladder One-Three-One—Stand by. Four Truck, Go ahead."
O'Callaghan: "What tower would you like us to respond into? Tower One or Tower Two? K."
Dispatcher: "Four Truck go to Two World Trade Center. K."

O'Callaghan:　"Four Truck—Ten-Four."[67]

Beside the coincidence of Ladder 4's and Ladder 131's fates intersecting and diverging by the chance that was one single second (If Lieutenant Wood had called one second earlier, would 131 have been sent straight to the South Tower instead of a staging area?) what strikes me most is O'Callaghan's tone of voice. He shows no hesitation or reluctance whatsoever, only a zeal to fulfill his duty. His final *Ten-Four* carries for an extra second as his voice raises slightly higher. He's ready.

They parked on Liberty Street, not far from the quarters of Engine 10 and Ladder 10 (across the street from the World Trade Center).[68]

**

Tim Brown was a firefighter detailed to the Office of Emergency Management. It was his job to coordinate interagency responses to large-scale incidents. [69] He arrived at the North Tower after the first plane struck in time to see his friends Chris Blackwell of Rescue 3 and Terry Hatton of Rescue 1. "This is bad, real bad," Blackwell told Brown. When the second tower was struck, Citywide Chief Donald Burns and Brown ran over to the South Tower lobby to coordinate what would be— in effect—an entire other rescue effort. Brown describes a woman running over to tell him about people stuck in an elevator. He followed her back to find an elevator car jammed with less than a foot space showing at the top of the open hoistway doors. It was full of people trapped. "The men were grabbing hold of the top of the doorway and trying to pull the car down," said Brown. "The base of the elevator shaft was full of burning jet fuel and the people were being barbequed—that's the only way I can describe it."[70]

Brown asked some Port Authority personnel to gather fire extinguishers but would soon learn that the extinguishers were ineffective against the jet fuel. "There I was in a hardhat and wearing a tie... But I felt like a fireman. I wished I had some tools to help them. But I didn't," Brown recalled. What he saw next would stay forever in his heart, especially in light of the allegations made later against Ladder 4. "At that very moment, I felt a tap on the shoulder. I turned and saw Mike Lynch."[71]

Tim Brown had worked with Michael Lynch in Ladder 4 years before and knew him well. He describes Lynch as one of the most talented and dedicated firemen he ever met.

"Timmy, I got this, Brother," said Lynch.

I got this may sound like a simple phrase but requires some explanation to those not familiar with firehouse jargon. At a fire or emergency, it is often necessary to say a lot with as few words as necessary. When you work with someone for years and know his capability, you develop a certain level of trust. When you feel about a brother firefighter the way Brown describes feeling about Michael Lynch, you have absolute trust in his ability. "I knew that 'I got this' meant everything that went along with getting those people out—his training and expertise, all of the tools and equipment on the rig, the fire, everything," said Brown. *I got this* said it all. "He may as well have had wings on his shoulders," said Brown. "It was like an angel arrived."[72]

Brown left the trapped people in the capable hands of 4 Truck because there were now radio reports of a third plane on the way. He made a phone call to Washington and then Albany to request air cover and then returned to Chief Burns.

The amount of injured people gathering in the lobby was growing and Burns wanted EMS personnel to begin transporting. He dispatched Brown to find a team of paramedics and Brown left the South Tower lobby only to find devastation outside.[73] "Jumpers were everywhere, a group of guys were huddled around Danny Suhr, who had just been hit," he told me, speaking of Firefighter Daniel Suhr who was killed when a jumper landed on him. While crossing the street, Brown heard a familiar voice calling out his name. "I turned to see Mike [Lynch] waving me over to help him with the Hurst Tool," Brown recalled.[74]

The Hurst Tool is a hydraulic extrication device— sometimes referred to as the Jaws of Life. The model in use in the FDNY in 2001 consisted of a very bulky and heavy power generator which pumped the hydraulic fluid to the spreader tools. It was a two-man job to carry the power unit. Lynch was attempting to pull the generator off Ladder 4's rig and called out to Brown for assistance. "I took a few steps toward him but then a probie showed up and grabbed the tool with him," said Brown. "I never saw Mike again."

The elevator was filled with employees of Keefe, Bruyette, and Woods and from Aon.[75] Linda Rothemund, of KBW had managed to squeeze through the opening and is almost certainly the woman who approached Tim Brown. In the time it took for Rothemund and Brown to return, Alan Mann of Aon had managed to slip out the tight opening and fell to the lobby floor, injured. Mann recalls stumbling across the lobby in search of assistance and eventually directing a group of firefighters back to the elevator.[76] Mann reportedly found the lobby empty and went down into the "shopping mall" to find firemen to help those still stuck in the elevator.[77] Because Linda Rothemund exited the elevator first and found Tim Brown, we know at least two firefighters were in the lobby at the time Mann escaped the elevator car (Brown and Burns). It is possible Mann did not see them but unlikely the firemen he found were Ladder 4, based on

Port Authority police radio transmissions of Lauren Smith's removal (beginning at 9:39 AM)[78] and Ladder 4's estimated arrival time, 9:30.[79] Nor is it unusual that firemen would have been found in the "shopping mall," or concourse level, as the concourse provided connection between the two tower lobbies and from other entrance points in the area with the benefit of protection from falling debris. Ladder 4, however, entered the South Tower lobby from the street level entrance on Liberty Street, as confirmed by multiple witnesses.

Tim Brown has no memory of seeing Mann near the elevator and must have arrived with Rothemund after Mann stumbled off. Sometime after the exchange between Brown and Lynch and Brown's leaving the elevator area, a woman named Lauren Smith, of KBW, managed to squeeze out of the tight opening and fell to the lobby floor. She lost her balance and fell into the open elevator shaft. She landed some ten feet down (where the fire was burning) and lay at the base injured.

"I was able to pull myself up using the cable and started screaming for help,"[80] Smith would recall. "Linda had already gotten some firemen. They pulled me out of there. They were trying to keep me still because they weren't sure if I'd injured my neck."[81]

Smith was pulled out of the shaft by a group of firefighters, later described as a "human ladder" [82] lowered down into the shaft. Security guards Ron Hoerner and James Flores, Port Authority cops and EMS workers improvised a crude stretcher out of a thick-glass desktop and carried Smith to an ambulance outside.[83] Because Lauren Smith was rescued after Tim Brown spoke to Mike Lynch, we know Ladder 4 was at the elevator during her removal. It is not known which members of Ladder 4 were lowered down into the shaft to rescue Smith. What is certain, based on Smith's later recollections, is that at the time she was carried out, Ladder 4 was still there (she remembers seeing them with the Hurst Tool) and any timeline reconstructed must account for the fact that Mike Lynch first entered the lobby, spoke with Tim Brown at the elevator, and then returned outside to the rig to get the Hurst Tool.

As she was being carried away, Lauren Smith looked back one last time. "I looked over and could see the firemen were using the jaws of life to try to get the elevator open."[84] She specifically remembers the "Jaws of Life." There is our smoking gun—no other company brought a Hurst Tool into the lobby.[85] What's more, Ladder 4 was operating the Hurst Tool—desperately trying to free the remaining trapped occupants of the elevator—up to the moment of their deaths. No sooner was Smith placed in an ambulance outside than the South Tower collapsed.[86]

Months later, Lauren Smith became determined to find out who the firemen were that rescued her. She visited the Engine 54/Ladder 4 firehouse to ask questions and look at pictures. Smith sat in the firehouse kitchen and told her story to the families of the men who died. They were brought to tears, relieved to hear confirmation of the men's final moments.[87]

**

When Michael Lynch's body was recovered, beside him was the Hurst Tool.[88] His last actions in life were carrying the "Jaws of Life" through a minefield of falling jumpers and making a desperate attempt to save those trapped people. The remains of the other Ladder 4 members were found in the same area—the crushed ruins of the South Tower lobby, by the elevator.[89] They died doing their duty.

"When I heard about what [Langewiesche] wrote, I immediately drove out to Long Island to see Denise," said

Brown describing his conversation with Lynch's wife. "I wanted his wife and kids to know that I was the only living person who saw what Mike did and that he died an American hero."[90]

There are, in fact, other living people who saw what Ladder 4 did. Captain Paul Mallery had just finished a 24-hour shift in Ladder 10 on the morning of September 11.[91] He was relieved by Lieutenant Steve Harrell, who would be killed shortly after. Engine 10 and Ladder 10's firehouse is on Liberty Street directly across from the World Trade Center. Mallery was preparing to do volunteer work for a political candidate's primary election later that morning and he hopped in the shower to get ready. He came out to hear a flurry of activity downstairs on the apparatus floor. Ladder 10 and Engine 10 had responded with their rigs and the empty apparatus floor was packed with civilians. Mallery quickly put his uniform back on and went to see what the fuss was about. "There were injured people everywhere," said Mallery. "Many of them horribly. One guy said 'I'm a paramedic,' and I pointed him towards the EMS locker and said 'There's your box of toys—go to work." [92] Mallery spent the next hour triaging patients and coordinating the firehouse's recall of off-duty members. As the second tower was struck and additional emergency personnel arrived, Mallery struggled to manage the impromptu resource center 10 House had become.

"I looked out to see 4 Truck turn off of West Street and come down Liberty. There was a raised crosswalk in the middle of the block and they drove over it. I worked in Ladder 110 [a Brooklyn company] and we used to do that in the Housing Projects—it can damage the rig—so I specifically remember them going over the crosswalk. They drove under the pedestrian bridge that led to the

Bankers' Trust building and parked near the entrance to 2 [the South Tower, 2 World Trade Center]."[93]

Mallery had a clear view of Ladder 4 as they got off the rig and grabbed their tools. "I remember the Can Man [firefighter assigned to carry an extinguisher] grabbing his six-foot hook and can –OK, I thought, they're going to work. They had to scramble to get in the building. I mean—they had to run for their lives. They were dodging things left and right." Mallery remembers the debris and falling bodies raining down on Liberty Street. The scene may have been frightening, but it did not deter the men of 4 Truck. "They got off the rig with a purpose," said Mallery. "I mean—no hesitation."[94]

We know Michael Lynch and at least one other member of Ladder 4 returned to the rig to retrieve the Hurst Tool.[95] The scene outside as described by Tim Brown and Paul Mallery was dire. One firefighter had already been killed by a falling body. To think the men of Ladder 4 would have made additional trips outside to the rig to stash stolen jeans is ludicrous. Mallery did not see the members of Ladder 4 come outside again before the South Tower collapsed.[96]

The timeline of events, as described by Smith, Brown and Mallery, does not even allow for the time it would have taken for the men of 4 Truck to get inside, descend the stairs to the concourse level into the shopping mall, find the Gap store (hundreds of feet away, at the foot of Building 6, closer to Vessey Street), load up with multiple stacks of jeans, and then climb back up to street level and brave the falling hell outside to put the jeans in the rig's crew cab. Even if one assumes Langewiesche meant the jeans came from the Structure or Express stores and not the Gap (Structure and Express were located in the lower concourse directly adjacent the South Tower), the timeline doesn't add up. It is important to remember, however, that Langewiesche specifically says the jeans were from the Gap—"tagged, folded, stacked by size."[97]

**

Langewiesche's description of the discovery of jeans inside Ladder 4's rig is straightforward. "Its crew cab was filled with dozens of new pairs of jeans from the Gap," he writes.[98] *American Ground* is written mostly in first person narrative; Langewiesche is describing what he saw. Later, responding to the controversy of this passage, he would admit that he did not witness the discovery of jeans on the rig but was repeating what was told to him by construction engineers.[99] He is within his rights to recount what was told to him by people he deemed credible. I would consider it unethical, however, to transition from events he witnessed to things he was told without clearly informing the reader he is departing from his own direct observation. There is no such advisory. The reader moves right through the events assuming Langewiesche witnessed them himself. Langewiesche explains his reason for including this story as his desire to show the discord between construction and fire personnel.[100] It would have been fairly easy to write something like: *Tensions were so high on the pile that construction workers would accuse fallen firefighters of stealing jeans. One construction foreman told me that when a fire truck was unearthed, stacked and folded jeans were found stashed inside.* It's not hard to write and it gets the point across without giving the reader a false sense of eyewitness account. I would also add that while this latter approach would have been more honest, I still feel it would be wrong to include it in any history of the World Trade Center recovery without including an investigation into the story's (i.e. the stealing of the jeans) veracity.

In later published versions of *American Ground,* the word "Gap" is omitted. Langewiesche instead writes that the rig contained "dozens of new pairs of jeans from a Trade Center store."§§§ (p. 160). This revision raises more questions than it answers. If Langewiesche were simply repeating what he was told, as he claimed in a subsequent interview,[101] then why would there be a need to change it? Was he not told "Gap"? Did his source have second thoughts—perhaps after learning the Gap was too far away for the story to be believable? In the afterword to the 2011 paperback edition, he repeats that he had been told "Gap" (p. 217). If he was told "Gap" and the passage is strictly what he was told,[102] then why change it? Another revision to the 2011 edition is the addition of the phrase "In their eyes." (p. 161). Originally written as "It was hard to avoid the conclusion..." [103] (2002), Langewiesche then writes, "In their eyes [the construction workers], it was hard to avoid the conclusion that the looting had begun even before the first tower fell..." (2011, p. 161). While this addition creates distance between the construction workers' conclusion and whatever Langewiesche's own conclusion might have been, it does little to atone for the original sin that was the passage's inclusion in the first place. First and foremost, the discovery of the jeans is still recounted in the same straightforward manner. The reader still assumes Langewiesche witnessed it as well. He could have fixed this in the later edition. He didn't.

**

There would not have been time for looting even if making a run for the jeans was all Ladder 4 did; and there definitely could not have been time when we know they were engaged in other activities, like pulling Lauren

---

§§§2011 paperback edition (Simon & Schuster).

Smith out of the elevator shaft and retrieving and operating the Hurst Tool. Author and journalist George Black, who specializes in historical reconstruction and has written for *The New Yorker, The New York Times, The Los Angeles Times* and many other publications, examined the physical evidence of Ladder 4's rig's location, its proximity to the Gap and the other stores, and eyewitness testimony. He also doubts that Ladder 4 would have had time for a looting expedition. Black argues that the approximate 30 minutes that transpired between Ladder 4's arrival and the South Tower collapse is a timeframe filled by 4 Truck members' actions witnessed at the elevator.[104]

Maps show the location of the Structure and Express stores—on the lower concourse level and directly next to the South Tower. Black points to these two stores as the most likely source of any jeans found in the vicinity— *vicinity* being the key word. The stores were, after all, smashed downward at the same time as Ladder 4's rig toward the same resting place levels below the surface. And as we will soon see, there were no jeans found *inside* Ladder 4's rig.

Patrick Drury is a cameraman who was hired by FEMA to document the World Trade Center rescue and recovery. He spent months documenting the operation. He was on the scene when Ladder 4's rig was uncovered. Almost 16 years after the events, I spoke with Drury about the night 4 Truck was dug out. "I was shocked how far down it was," he told me, speaking about the rig's final resting place. He described being as surprised as anyone by Langewiesche's description of events that night. His footage was known about even at the time but interest in it gained little traction. "CBS interviewed me about it," he said. "I don't know what came of it."[105] Drury released a

written statement about his experience. I think it
warrants a full reading:

> After the attacks on September 11th at the World Trade
> Center I was hired by FEMA to document the recovery
> effort after FEMA's video units were removed from New
> York City. Our job was to walk the site as often as FEMA
> deemed necessary in order to document the changes at
> the site for release to various news agencies and for
> archival purposes.
>
> The evening that Ladder 4 was discovered was very
> cold and rainy. We had already been walking the pit for
> a few hours documenting the work that was going on
> and the changes that had occurred since our last visit
> when we made our way towards the South East corner
> of the site. At first, I was hesitant to approach the area
> not knowing exactly why so many firemen had
> converged at this location. I could only assume that they
> had found another body, presumably one of their own.
> We kept our distance for a while as one of our FEMA
> escorts broke away from our group to find out what was
> happening. After a few minutes I was told that a ladder
> truck had been found and that the firemen were trying
> to recover the driver's body from the cab. The
> gentleman from our group returned and told me that the
> firemen were OK with me shooting them as they
> searched for their colleague. I later learned from the
> firemen that they were very upset about the cutbacks
> that Mayor Giuliani had just made decreasing the
> number of firefighters allowed to work and search the
> site. They were happy to let me shoot this recovery
> because they wanted people to see that they were still
> finding their brothers and that their time was well spent
> and necessary. With this in mind, I stood in the rain and
> the trade center muck with the firemen and we all
> looked on as a few of their own dug with their hands and
> small tools in order to get to the truck's cab. After fifteen
> minutes they got into the cab and we all watched hoping
> that they would find the driver. A glove was pulled out

and then a few scraps of cloth that looked as if they might have once been a pair of pants or a jacket. Shortly there after a fireman on the other side of the cab popped his head up over the vehicle and said that there were no remains to be found. The mood was very somber and I could feel the strain on the men around me. The group around Ladder 4 began to disperse and everyone returned to their section of the disaster to continue working.

Months later when I heard of the controversy surrounding this event I was shocked. I could not believe that someone had reported that jeans from the Gap had been found in the cab of Ladder 4 or that they had been strewn about for several days for all to see. If this had been the case I would have had one of the biggest stories to come out of the World Trade Center since its destruction. As a cameraman it is my job to absorb and capture all the details of whatever I am shooting. There is to be no bias or censoring of what I shoot. If there had been Gap Jeans in the cab of Ladder 4 and all around it as it laid 6 stories below street level I would have gladly shot them. If there are any doubts of these facts all one has to do is review the FEMA footage.[106]

The scene Drury described is nothing like Lagewiesche's account—where construction workers cheered upon discovering stacks of jeans inside the cab. "Jeans! Look at these! Fucking guys! Jeans!" [107] construction workers are reported to have said—giddy with having found the long sought after proof of the firemen's transgressions. I have seen Drury's footage (available online). It is indeed a very somber scene. There are no cheering construction workers and there are no jeans. Perhaps the most important thing missing from the video footage is any sign of William Langewiesche.

**

Firefighter Don Schneider was also present at the unearthing of Ladder 4's rig and—aside from the surreal sight of a fire truck smashed underground—he doesn't remember "anything spectacular" about the operation.[108] "I didn't see anything in the rig," recalled Schneider, when asked about the presence of jeans in the crew cab. He, after all, was more concerned with human remains than wrecked trucks. Schneider looked inside the cab and then went off to find another place to dig.[109] "I moved on once there were no bodies [inside the cab]," Schneider explained. In contrast to Langewiesche's depiction of construction workers taunting firefighters and reveling in the triumph of stumbling upon the dead firemen's loot, Schneider describes the equipment operators and tradesmen as simply waiting for the firefighters to get out of their way.[110] "There was no confrontation."[111]

CHAPTER 11

IN THE SPAN OF A FEW DAYS I read *American Ground* from cover to cover. There were many parts I found very interesting. I had been a young firefighter at the World Trade Center site with only the narrow view that my low rank and position allowed. I knew nothing of the strategy meetings of the upper managers of the scene. I was a grunt. The behind-the-scenes wrangling and daily drama that went into the recovery and clean up of that enormous tragedy fascinated me. There were also parts of the book that made my blood boil. Langewiesche describes the mentality of the rescue and recovery workers as "tribal." Each tribe—firemen, police (both city and Port Authority), and construction—fiercely protected their own turf and viewed the other tribes with suspicion.[112] This was undeniably true. Reading *American Ground,* I could not help but to revert back to my own tribal instincts and as I did, the restless anger resurfaced and I could not sleep for days. I do not blame Langewiesche for my sleepless nights. Instead, I ask myself why I needed him to be wrong.

When *American Ground* was released in 2002, I read only the passages that pertained to Ladder 4 and went straight past denial to anger. My anger was fueled by the certainty that Langewiesche was just some yellow journalist tossing cheap shots from the sidelines of history—'the critic outside the arena,' to quote Teddy Roosevelt. He was not.

William Langewiesche spent more time at the World Trade Center site than I did. Not only did he crash the big meetings, he shadowed inspection teams and went along on expeditions into the depths of twisted hell. In short, he was an embedded journalist covering a war on the frontlines. He had angered me greatly back in 2002 with his allegations, partly because they served to pick at the emotional wounds of my entire 9/11 experience. But time softened my anger and Pellegrino's work allowed me to rest assured that John Tipping and Ladder 4 would be acquitted by posterity. The questions about Pellegrino's integrity shook me out of this security. I needed a new reassurance and I decided I was going to have to create it myself. The first step was to read the full text of *American Ground*. With every page came further proof that Langewiesche was not the simple yellow journalist I had dismissed him as. He spoke with authority—which complicated things.

As difficult as it was to read the parts of *American Ground* I knew to be inaccurate, I found it harder to read the passages where I knew he got it right. His description of the "jealous sense of ownership" that all involved with the recovery felt for their own losses stands out.[113] Emotions were indeed raw, as Langewiesche points out. Everyone involved felt the tragedy had happened to them personally and the closer the loss—coworker, best friend, parent, brother or sister, son or daughter—the more it felt like your own tragedy more than someone else's (someone who hadn't lost someone as close as you did). Langewiesche does not limit this phenomenon to firefighters, but does add that "firemen in particular felt that they had a special relationship with the site, not only because they had lost 343 people there... but also because afterward their survivors, along with their dead, had been idolized as national heroes, and subjected to the full force of modern publicity."[114] He then points out, correctly, that some firefighters behaved "embarrassingly" under such adulation. Most did not (as even Langewiesche concedes), but there are always exceptions. It was indeed a small minority of firefighters who acted poorly, and under such an intense spotlight certain things can be misunderstood. A fireman posing for a photo with a visitor at the site's border may seem like "grandstanding" at first, but could have been an act of kindness to a genuine, emotional request from a well-wisher. Still, the reminder of the handful of firefighters who stood out as less than modest irked me, if only because their actions could be used as justification for other, unfair, characterizations.

**

If Langewiesche was not just some cheap hustler peddling lies to sell books—the *vulture,* as I had called him—then what was he? As I moved further into *American Ground* and regressed deeper into my tribal loyalties, I found the answer. He was a journalist. One with unlimited access to the operation—access granted by Holden and facilitated by chief engineers. With a front row seat to their exploits and a constant ear to their frustrations, his perspective was naturally exposed to a greater degree to their viewpoint, regardless of any professional objectivity he may have tried to cling to. Langewiesche *was* correct in his description of the tribal mentality at the site. He just failed to recognize, or anyway admit, that he belonged to the tribe of the construction workers/engineers. This was only natural and I would not suggest that it makes his reporting any less valid. He was certainly professional enough not to gloss over the engineers' faults, nor the shortcomings of the cops at the site. But he is never as vicious in his criticism of the other "tribes" as he is with the firemen.

Certainly the firefighters at the World Trade Center had their faults, but Langewiesche often takes kernels of truth—interpreted by someone with an axe to grind—and portrays it as indisputable fact. Folded jeans near a buried fire truck become folded jeans inside a buried fire truck and *voilà*—smoking gun. Throughout *American Ground,* there were many such examples.

In the opening pages Langewiesche describes a "widespread pattern of looting that started even before the towers fell."[115] He at first lays equal blame on cops, firemen, and construction workers and offers some dumped out purses and dust outlines on desks where computers had stood (inside the doomed Bankers Trust building across the street from the Twin Towers) as proof.[116] The items probably were stolen, but in the context of the first few weeks after the attacks in which Langewiesche himself describes a chaos of thousands of emergency personnel, construction and support workers, civilian volunteers, and outright gawkers descending on the scene, it hardly seems possible to assign blame. He would return to this theme of looting many times, often as a counterargument to the narrative that firefighters at the World Trade Center—before and after the collapses—were heroic. "Firemen were said to prefer watches from the Torneau store,"[117] Langewiesche writes in one passage in which he also describes the looting preferences of cops and construction workers.[118] *Said to prefer.* Who did the saying is left to the reader's imagination.

With the exception of bottles of water and such taken—out of dire necessity—from an already heavily damaged store on the first day, I can honestly say I did not witness a single act of looting in all my time at the World Trade Center site. It would be foolish of me, however, to think it did not happen. I'm sure it did. My objection is with Langewiesche's use of the words "widespread pattern."

Firehouse culture is a powerful force. Long held traditions are passed down from one generation to the next, and there is a great deal of peer pressure to fall in line. One deeply felt tradition is that responding to someone's emergency is a sacred trust. We respond to people's homes often when they are at their most vulnerable state and we pride ourselves in doing it faithfully. Even if a firefighter—who was overhauling after a fire and noticed some jewelry on the dresser—had no moral or legal qualms about slipping it in his pocket, he would be terrified that another member of his company saw him do it. He would be an outcast in his firehouse and his days on the job would be numbered. In a department with over eleven thousand active firefighters, I'm sure there can be a tiny percentage of bad apples who may break their sacred trust despite this enormous peer pressure, but certainly not enough to create an organized system that includes a preferred watch store. And definitely not enough for an entire company of firefighters to disregard calls for help during the greatest scene of devastation our city has ever seen and casually carry stacks of jeans past a command post full of dozens of staged firemen and hide them in the rig parked outside.

It is also worth noting that Johnny Dunham, a 26-year old unemployed security guard from the Bronx, was arrested and subsequently pleaded guilty to impersonating a firefighter and stealing thousands of dollars worth of watches from the very Torneau store in question. [119] By November, *The New York Post* had reported a dozen arrests of imposters caught stealing from the Trade Center site, many of whom were wearing stolen FDNY gear and helmets.[120] There is no mention of this in *American Ground.*

"Firemen were said to prefer..." Obviously the people doing the saying were the people Langewiesche had most access to. As we have seen, they were people with reasons (some justified, some not) to resent the firefighters' presence at the site. In a 2002 interview on *NPR,* Langewiesche explains: "This particular story [of the jeans on Ladder 4's rig] was told to me, was reported to me by people who I had known and worked with closely for months who were very level-headed people, who were there, who had proved to be, you know, very reliable."[121] The *well-respected* man at the center of his story is a construction foreman whom Langewiesche describes as having wished he could throw all of the firemen off the site. His list of grievances include how he "especially didn't like the fact that they kept forcing his operation to shut down—once for three days straight—while they worked by hand and poked through the rubble for their colleagues' remains."[122]

Very level-headed indeed.

**

Langewiesche does not limit his criticism of the Fire Department to looting allegations. As I have already discussed, the media attention directed toward firemen was enormous. Stories of firefighters' 'heroics' were ubiquitous and constant, and were, in fact, to the neglect of other stories of true bravery arising from the attacks. Langewiesche faults the public for doling out such unabashed praise to firefighters but blames the firemen even more so for playing into it.

One could look at the missteps of some members of a group with no prior experience in handling such adulation, deserved or not. Or, one could look at the countless acts of deference and humble demurral. The highest example of this can be found in the actions of the three—undoubtedly—most famous firefighters who have ever lived. Outside of the FDNY, few know their names, but their image has been seen the world over. I am talking, of course, about the three men who raised the American flag atop the pile of Trade Center debris and were immortalized by Thomas E. Franklin's photograph.[123] The picture has been seen in newspapers and magazines across the globe. It was even featured on a postage stamp. The three firefighters, George Johnson, Dan McWilliams, and Billy Eisengrein, could have made millions of dollars and turned their famous image into fulltime careers as celebrities. But they didn't. They formed a charity and gave what money they earned from the photo to others in need.[124] For years, the three men did virtually no interviews about the photograph.

Look at the men from Rescue 4, Squad 270 and Ladder 111 who were so vital to the rescue of John McLoughlin. They have never sought nor received acknowledgment in any way. To my knowledge, this book is the first time any of their names have been mentioned publicly at all in regard to McLoughlin's rescue. The police officers involved in the rescue each received their respective agencies' highest medals for valor, and deservedly so. No Fire Department member requested nor received any medal for any rescues (and there were many) at the World Trade Center. In fact, the annual awarding of medals scheduled for June 2002 (which would have covered 2001) was canceled. The Fire Department gave out no medals for *any* rescues in 2001. There was no mood for celebration. Canceling such an event—and refusing of all accolades from World Trade Center rescues—is a big decision made at the highest levels but also one that was almost unanimously supported by the rank and file.

When bestowing of the word hero was within firefighters' control, more often than not they declined. We cannot help it if the media had other ideas and some members of the Fire Department may have gotten caught up in the barrage of praise. Most did not.

Frustration with the media's need to create sensationalized heroes in the easiest terms without painting a true picture of the countless acts of bravery by many, many people does not justify an almost complete dismissal of any courage whatsoever in the Fire Department's response to the attacks. Langewiesche acknowledges a few acts of bravery, after the first collapse, by firemen who stayed in the North Tower lobby to help civilians, but dismisses all other firefighters who died that day as "unintentional martyrs, noncombatants, typical casualties of war."[125] Those who died in the South Tower collapse were killed without warning and most who died in the North Tower were on the upper floors in stairwells with no knowledge of the other tower's collapse or impending danger, by his estimate.[126]

"They were not soldiers crossing the lip of a trench or assaulting a machine-gun nest in battle," Langewiesche points out, as if citing an example from history of someone he feels was more brave highlights how less brave the firefighters were. He sees few heroics in "climbing endless stairwells one flight at a time in the company of friends, and with little obvious purpose in mind beyond finding the civilians who must have been injured by the twin attacks."[127] Many firefighters did in fact die while climbing stairs. I still find an admirable bravery in dying while going toward the danger—dying in the attempt to help others. And while the sacrifice of these firefighters' deaths needs no justification, there is surviving evidence of what many firefighters were doing at the moment they were cut down.[128]

Battalion Chief Orio Palmer was assigned to the 7th Battalion, in Chelsea, and was sent to take command of the main fire floor (point of impact), the 78th floor, of the South Tower. All of the elevators in the South Tower were impacted by the attack, but Palmer, his aide Stephen Belson, and the members of Ladder 15, led by Lieutenant Joseph Leavey,**** were able to repair a service elevator that reached the 40th floor. One member of Ladder 15 was left to operate the elevator while the rest of the crew began climbing from the 40th to the 78th floor. [129] Handie-talkie transmissions between Chief Palmer and Ladder 15 were recorded by Port Authority repeaters. The recordings offer a heartwrenching glimpse into the final moments of men determined to save as many people as they could.

"We've got two isolated pockets of fire. We should be able to knock it down with two [hose] lines,"[130] Palmer tells Leavey. He goes on to describe "numerous ten-forty-fives, code ones," the fire radio code for fatal victims. Along with Battalion Chief Edward Geraghty, Palmer was able to locate a set of access stairs between the 78th and 79th floors.[131] Access stairs are open stairwells between floors occupied by a common tenant (not the enclosed exit stairwells). Many office buildings with tenants occupying multiple floors have access stairs. In this case, the significance of the discovery was huge. The impact of the plane into the South Tower severed all of the stairwells, trapping anyone above the impact zone above

---

****The members of Ladder 15 killed on 9/11 were Lieutenant Joseph Leavey, Firefighters Richard Allen, Arthur Barry, Thomas Kelly, Scott Kopytko, Scott Larsen, Douglas Oelschlager, and Eric Olsen.

the fire.†††† The fact that Palmer and Geraghty had found a way to get people down from the floors above the fire could have saved hundreds, if they'd only had more time.

Meanwhile, the men of Ladder 15 had stretched two "house" lines on the 78th floor. House lines are hoses, usually stored in tin boxes next to the standpipe, found in the stairwells of high-rise buildings. They are usually of low quality and firefighters avoid using them. Being a ladder company (carrying rescue tools instead of hose lines), 15 Truck was left with little choice. If they wanted to knock down some fire before an engine company could get up there, they needed to use the house lines. The water pressure must have been pathetic. The standpipes themselves were most likely severed by the impact, so supply from engine pumpers connected to hydrants in the street would have been useless. The only water would have come from what remained in the pipe and water tanks on the roof. Regardless of these challenges, the members of Ladder 15 advanced into the fire with what water they had. Leavey transmits their progress to Palmer, calmly adding that they were trapped by fire and would be temporarily delayed. [132] Chiefs Palmer and Geraghty, and the men of 15 Truck were doing their best to push back fire just enough so people could come down the access stairs. The recordings stop soon after—the moment the South Tower collapses. These men did not die with "little obvious purpose in mind." They were faced with hell and they were making a stand.

I do not feel that the death of a firefighter who arrived at the scene of the burning towers and—faithful to his duty—went in to do his job is any more tragic than the

---

††††One stairwell in the South Tower was left partially passable and a small handful of people did escape from above the fire. Most, however, were unable to find a way past the impact floors.

death of a dishwasher from Windows on the World, or a broker from Cantor Fitzgerald, or a fire safety director from the Port Authority, or anyone else. All of the lives lost were precious and by virtually all survivors' accounts, in every situation where somebody needed help evacuating, their fellow citizens—coworker and stranger alike—stepped up to help. The fact that many people displayed great courage that day does not mean the firefighters displayed none (or most firefighters according to Langewiesche). They were not lambs being led to the slaughter or "unintentional martyrs."

Langewiesche's sympathy for those who resented the overblown hero worship being showered onto firemen blinds him to the conscious sacrifice of nearly all of the first responders who died that day. There are numerous videos available of fire units arriving at the scene of the attacks. One that I find particularly moving features the arrival of Squad 288.[133] They responded from Queens and therefore arrived well into the operation. The camera zooms in as they approach the exterior wall of the building to avoid falling debris and jumpers from the upper floors. The expressions on their faces are discernable. They are worried, as I would have been. They forge ahead, however, and enter one of the towers. They all died. There was nothing unintentional about their perseverance.

Terry Hatton was the captain of Rescue 1. He spent most of his career in rescue companies and it's fair to say—in his two decades on the job—he saw a considerable amount of carnage and danger. Upon entering the lobby of Tower 1 with his company, Hatton came across his old friend, Firefighter Tim Brown. The two men embraced and Hatton said, "I love you, brother. It might be the last time I see you."[134] The men of Rescue 1 knew what they were walking into. They all died.

If Langewiesche does not believe the average firefighter's death on 9/11 resulted from any kind of conscious sacrifice on his part, he definitely refutes the notion that the firemen involved in the rescue and recovery effort were exhibiting any kind of selfless bravery. He points out the obvious that the firemen on the pile either survived the collapse or had not been in the buildings when they fell. "But if the loss of the others was to mean anything beyond the waste of war," he adds, "it had to be admitted that people on the pile since then, though ferociously dedicated to a grim and dangerous task, were simply not involved in heroics." [135] Langewiesche bemoans the public portrayal that "conditions on the pile were so difficult that merely by working there the people were sacrificing themselves."[136] He points out, probably correctly, that the lion's share of this narrative was directed toward firemen.

I agree with Langewiesche on this point. Simply being on the pile did not make anyone a hero. It was physically exhausting and emotionally draining, but not heroic. At the end of the day, it was our job—a job we volunteered for. There was dignity, however, in the search for remains. As Langewiesche notes, 1,209 individuals' remains were identified in the first ten months after the attacks.[137] That's 1,209 families that were given at least the most basic sense of closure. Most guys I know who worked at the site shun the word hero. But every recovery worker can own the dignity of reuniting a family with a loved one's remains. If there is a strong sense of pride in this dignity, it should not be mistaken for reveling in perceived heroics, whatever the outside world may have presented the recovery work as. Langewiesche may have had a point, but he does his argument no favors by juxtaposing it with his often mythical descriptions of chief engineers and construction managers on the pile—

where their presence inspired results in a place so dangerous one manager said "he would be very surprised if no one got killed."[138] Construction workers, police officers, and firefighters each faced dangers at the site and it is true that the work of construction workers was less touted by the media and public—an oversight Langewiesche rightly tries to correct. The extention of his effort to praise chief engineers and construction managers into unfair attacks on firefighters, however, reveals his loss of objectivity. He's fighting for his tribe.

And while I, like Langewiesche, would not have called the recovery work heroic, history may have proven us both wrong. In the 16-plus years since the World Trade Center attacks, hundreds of first responders and recovery workers have died as a result of 9/11 illnesses and thousands are sick.

Further proof of Langewiesche's loss of objectivity in favor of the construction managers and chief engineers lies in two examples. First is the matter of pay scales. While he does concede that none of the workers at the site were primarily motivated by money, he mentions as a matter of course that the equipment operators were being paid at a rate of $200k per year[139] (this is the figure he provides, I do not know what they were paid). To ensure no one would think the construction "tribe" was given unfair reward compared to uniformed personnel, Langewiesche states that cops and firemen at the site were there on overtime.[140] I cannot speak for the police. Firemen, however, were not there on overtime, with certain exceptions. In the first few days, when an on-duty company was dispatched directly to the site—and then returned to their firehouse after their shift ended—there may have been some overtime incurred. But many of the firefighters on the pile in the first few weeks were there on their own time—in between their shifts at the firehouse. [‡‡‡‡] And once the recovery became more organized, the search for remains at the site was done by firefighters detailed to the Trade Center for 30-day rotations, earning their regular pay. There may have been a handful of firefighters with special training and expertise who were assigned on a more permanent basis earning some overtime, I do not know—but if there were, they weren't the majority. The expertise provided by most of the Special Operations Command came in the form of the daily dispatched rescue and squad companies (working their regular tours).

It is true that there was a lot of overtime elsewhere for firefighters during the months after 9/11. Firehouse rosters were decimated and there were numerous special events and security details to staff. I couldn't care less about who was paid what at the Trade Center; no firefighter I know went down there for the money. But it is disingenuous to give the impression that firefighters at the site were paid handsomely as a buffer to any sympathy the reader may feel compelled to give.

The other example is found in Langewiesche's description of the all around ugly episode of a scuffle between protesting firefighters and police on November 2. In his account, firefighters—unhappy about the plan to scale back the number of rescue workers at the site—rioted and attacked police officers.[141] He is not only critical of the firefighters' actions, but also dismissive of their motives. It is just further evidence, for Langewiesche, that firemen were out of control.

[‡‡‡‡]Some active and retired firefighters continued to work at the site on their own time throughout the recovery effort, including many who had lost family members in the attacks. A group of fathers who had lost their firefighter sons, including Lee Ielpi, John Vigiano—who lost two sons, one a fireman and the other a cop—and many others comprised a constant cohort at the site.

Best-selling author (and former firefighter) Dennis Smith recorded the events in his book *Report from Ground Zero*. Smith also spent months chronicling the rescue and recovery efforts and, needless to say, his version of events is quite different than Langewiesche's. Smith describes the front-line police officers at the demonstration as sympathizing with the firefighters— who were making a genuine plea to stop what would have been a drastic reduction in rescue workers.[142] They did not want the Trade Center turned into a demolition site, with all remaining debris (and human remains) shipped off hurriedly to the landfill. Only when higher ranking police commanders ordered them to, did the cops arrest firefighters.[143]

I was not at the protest, but I've interviewed some of the arrested firemen. The demonstration was planned as a prayer gathering at the Trade Center site before a march to City Hall to air grievances. Barriers had been set up to keep the firefighters out and when the crowd overflowed the barriers, the police commanders intervened and ordered the cops to make arrests. This is where it got ugly.

"We were on the end of the line," one of the firemen told me.[144] "And then people yelled back for us to turn. The end of the line then became the front of a new line and we were pushed from behind across the barriers. The regular cops didn't do anything, but a police captain came and grabbed my arm hard."

Smith describes one cop being ordered to handcuff a fireman only to remove the cuffs when the commander wasn't looking.[145] "Later, an [other] officer who was driving the handcuffed fire Captain Jack Ginty to the police station became so upset over the senselessness of the event that he had to pull his car over to the side of the road to bring his sobbing under control."[146]

The firemen who crossed the barrier were arrested. Arrested for entering a site they had entered numerous times over the past month and a half at will—for entering the site to say a prayer. Emotions were already high and the sight of firefighters being handcuffed only made matters worse. One of the barriers was pushed into the police officers—which was wrong no matter what. The arrests, however, had begun before the barrier was pushed.[147]

Langewiesche describes the demonstration as culminating with a march to City Hall where the firefighters chanted for the ouster of Rudy Giuliani and Fire Commissioner Thomas Von Essen.[148] He describes the commissioner as someone "who for years had been a well-liked New York fireman and union leader," [and was only now being attacked for] "going around quietly making the point that by far the greatest loss of life had been civilian, and that the Trade Center tragedy was larger than just a firefighters' or even a New Yorkers' affair."[149] Thomas Von Essen had been fire commissioner for six years. He was opinionated and hands-on in his leadership of the FDNY and many of his decisions were unpopular with the rank and file. There were decisions he made that I disagreed with, but there were also good things that I gave him credit for. Whether you argue that Von Essen's unpopularity within the uniformed ranks was deserved or not, it would be untrue to say that he was "well-liked." He was always a polarizing figure among firemen. So, Langewiesche's assertion that the firefighters suddenly turned on their leader in continuance of an unruly and irrational tantrum is inaccurate. Whether they agreed or not, any firefighter in the city—if asked—could have told him why firemen were upset with the commissioner. Were any asked?

Most of the arrested firefighters were not charged with rioting or assault, but harassment and trespassing.§§§§ There was ample video of the demonstration and the District Attorney would not have let the assault of police officers slide. A total of 18 firefighters were ultimately arrested following the demonstration. After much back and forth between City Hall and the District Attorney's office, the charges were all dropped.[150] The issue at hand really was the recovery. There were still plenty of human remains to be discovered in the debris. The firefighters were sure of it and they would be proven right. In the end, the mayor compromised and the number of firefighters and police officers at the site was restored.[151]

The one firefighter Langewiesche praises is Sam Melisi.[152] Melisi was a veteran of the Special Operations Command who was detailed to the World Trade Center site for the duration of the rescue and recovery. I've met Sam Melisi but do not know him well. Close friends of mine have worked with him, however, and by all accounts he is the dedicated, knowledgeable, and level-headed man Langewiesche describes. In *American Ground*, unfortunately, Melisi is presented very much as the exception to the irrational, self-centered, boorish firefighters basking in public's adoration and buying into their own inflated sense of loss.[153] Melisi is the only firefighter Langewiesche writes about as having known on any kind of personal level and it makes me, as a reader and a firefighter, wish he could have known more. He would have learned that there were far more people like

---

§§§§One firefighter would be charged with assaulting a police officer, though the prosecutor would later state "It appears that the officer was pushed into the barricade due to the size and force of the crowd as a whole rather than by the act of any individual defendant," (see endnote 150). All charges against all the arrested firefighters were eventually dismissed.

Sam Melisi in the Fire Department than the type who behaved badly at the site and distorted his view. Melisi's unassuming professionalism was the norm, not the exception.

At the very moments of the tensest stand-offs at the Trade Center site, elsewhere in the city was Gerry Sweeney sitting up late nights to comfort grieving parents; there was Gus Rallis working past his guilt to adapt to the job that was drastically different than the one he had signed up for just a few months before. Indeed, at the other end of the pile were guys like Lee Ielpi standing out, overnight, in the cold and rain, raking through debris, hoping against the odds to bring home a loved one. None of these firemen were doing anything that lots of other people weren't doing. Cops, firefighters, office workers, construction workers—they all have their stories. I write this book to tell the firefighters' story—at least from my point of view—and hopefully a more complete story than the one offered in *American Ground.* And while I have dedicated much of this chapter to a number of Langewiesche's claims, it is not the scope of this work to simply counterargue—point by point— *American Ground.* I have laid out a series of assertions by an author whom I would argue was biased by the chief engineers' and construction managers' points of view for the purpose of showing how *American Ground's* greatest injustice came to be.

Certainly, there were examples of firefighters who behaved poorly—as there were with *every* group at the site. But by Langewiesche's account, the chief engineers' and construction managers' biggest problem with firefighters was that they kept stopping the dismantling and clean up work in order to recover human remains.[154] The two forces were never going to be compatible. A quicker clean up meant fewer remains recovered at the site and a painstaking search for and recovery of remains meant a slower clean up. It has never been explained to me in a satisfactory way what the rush was anyway. The clean up took nine months and you could argue that dragging it on toward the one-year mark would have been a bad thing (economically or emotionally). But what would have been gained by finishing the clean up in say—six months? Many more remains would have been further desecrated and found less intact, if at all, at the Staten Island Landfill. And what for? The hole left in the ground by the clean up stayed vacant for the better part of a decade afterward. For many reasons, there was certainly no rush to rebuild. Regardless, the engineers running the clean up were used to schedules and deadlines. Firefighters don't work with arbitrary deadlines—however long an extrication takes, it takes.

On top of the inevitable slowdowns for extricating remains, there was the century-old Fire Department tradition of firefighters carrying out their own dead. These additional delays would add to the chief engineers' frustrations and be the source of yet another criticism of firefighters at the site.

This particular criticism—that firefighters gave greater attention and respect to their own dead than to others—deserves some discussion. There is truth to it. The full answer, however, is highly nuanced and will ultimately depend on the critic's point of view. Since firemen were first organized into a paid department in the nineteenth century, there has been a heartfelt tradition that should one of our own be killed at a fire or collapse, he or she will not be left behind. We will do what it takes to bring our fallen brother or sister home. Whenever possible (during an extended recovery operation, for example) the other members of that firefighter's company will carry him or her out. So, in effect, firefighters at the World Trade Center site were carrying out a dual mission: Their professional duty as first responders to the citizens of New York (i.e. to recover the victims of the attack); and their time-honored tradition of bringing home their fallen brothers. I would argue that the police officers working the recovery were doing the same. There is nothing inherently wrong with this as long as both missions are carried out faithfully. Obviously, a tragedy which involves colleagues, close friends, or worst of all family will trigger a greater degree of emotions, but I don't think any critic—Langewiesche, the engineers, or anyone—would fault one of the firemen who lost a son for treating the recovery of his boy with greater reverence, for example. There were many examples like that, however, and it could have distorted perception.

Overall, though, I would say it was the higher percentage of firefighters' remains found relatively intact that would lead to the perception that firemen only cared for their own. The bunker gear the firefighters were wearing served to keep their bodies together to a much higher degree than police uniforms and civilian attire—a point Langewiesche concedes. "Generally, the bodies that endured best were those of firemen, because they were wrapped in equipment and heavy clothing," he explains.[155] By and large, civilians' remains were found in pieces and quite often not near other pieces. It was my experience that small parts of human remains (a foot, a finger, a piece of bone or skin for example) found— alone—were treated as evidence and bagged and removed as such. Larger sets of remains, be it simply bigger parts of the body or a grouping of smaller remains were given more attention and possibly body-bagged as one victim. So by shear numbers, many more firefighters were found and removed as a single body than were civilians. The bunker gear ensured a higher likelihood.

It is a true statement that recovery work rarely stopped completely (site-wide) for the removal of small body parts. Excavation with heavy equipment may have been halted in the immediate area of the remains to determine the amount. Then—if determined to be a small amount—they were usually bagged as evidence and their location was recorded by GPS equipment. It is important to remember that firefighters had no way of knowing whose body parts these were. Statistically speaking, there was a greater than 10 percent chance they belonged to a dead firefighter and I only mention this to rebut the argument that firefighters would have treated these parts differently if they were their own dead. Larger, more intact bodies (civilian, police, or fire) were treated more solemnly (within the context that *all* of the recoveries—small parts and whole bodies—were solemn occasions even if just private ones). A relatively intact body was put in a body bag and carried out on a stretcher by a group of impromptu pallbearers. Such carry-outs often involved the shutting down of all equipment on site and the lining up of all recovery workers.

The situation was complicated further by the issue of identification. Firefighters' bunker gear was marked with their name. It was fairly easy to figure out who the dead firefighter was and what firehouse he worked in. Furthermore, that firehouse was usually no more than a half-hour or 45 minute's drive away and they were open 24 hours a day. In sum, it was a manageable proposition to have the dead firefighter's company come carry him out. This was also true of police officers, who could be identified by their badges. Civilians' remains were almost never identifiable. Rarely were the remains large enough and even when they were, the bodies were unrecognizable and had nothing attached by which to identify them. This resulted in fewer carry-outs of civilian bodies. Even when a civilian's remains were substantial and carried out on a stretcher, there was no way to identify the body and notify loved ones who may have wanted to come participate in the carry-out. Even without on-site identification and notification of family, dead civilians were carried out with honor.

"At some point early yesterday morning," a *New York Times* reporter noted, "—when breaks in the smoky billows revealed a crescent moon—a body was pulled from the rubble, and firefighters rushed forward to see if a colleague had been found. It was a man whom no one recognized, wearing a white shirt, black pants and a wedding ring. Some of the firefighters cried as they eased the corpse into a body bag and carried it away. 'He was married, man,' was all that one could say. 'He was married.'"[156] The significance of *every* life lost was not lost on firefighters.

Still, as the months dragged on, an observer could easily assume that firefighters treated their own dead differently out of callousness. When work on the pile stopped and everyone lined up to pay respects to a body on a stretcher being carried out, it was usually a firefighter's body. Bunker gear skewed the statistics to ensure it.

Langewiesche touches on this theme often, usually while relaying the chief engineers' criticisms of firefighters. He also describes how chief engineers and construction managers would have preferred to bulldoze the entire pile into barges more quickly and sort out the remains at the Staten Island Landfill.[157] I have already stated my belief that the charge of firefighters caring only about their own dead is a distorted view, but for the moment let's assume it was true. What moral authority would the engineers—in Langewiesche's account—have in condemning the firefighters' special reverence for *some* of the dead when they themselves held special reverence for *none* of the dead? To be clear, *I* am not claiming the chief engineers or construction managers disregarded the importance of recovering human remains at the site. I did not deal with the higher ups on the construction side; but the working guys I met (operating engineers, iron workers etc.) gave us no grief about stopping to extricate remains. In fact they were always helpful. I am simply pointing out the paradox of Langewiesche's narrative. How can engineers simultaneously complain about firefighters slowing down their work and also criticize firefighters for not having slowed it down even more?

The answer to that question is not important. It is enough to take Langewiesche at his word when he states that the decision makers on the construction side resented the firefighters' presence for all of the reasons stated above. The groundwork was laid for a vicious and exaggerated story to take root and be given credence by people with their own reasons for wanting it to be true.

"Imagine [the construction superintendent's] delight, then, after the hulk of the fire truck appeared, that rather than containing bodies (which would have required decorum), its crew cab was filled with dozens of new pairs of jeans from the Gap, a Trade Center store,"[158] writes Langewiesche. Aside from the fact that we now know there were no jeans found in the crew cab of Ladder 4, this passage tells much about both the mentality of the construction manager involved and Langewiesche's partiality for not having challenged the superintendent's story. Delight is a strong word. If it were true that Ladder 4 died in the act of looting, it would have been cause for sadness and anger, not delight.

The bitterness arising from the rivalries and grievances described above made conditions ripe for the bombshell accusation that firefighters committed the unforgivable act of abandoning the trapped victims they had been dispatched to save for the luster of free denim. Reports of firefighters looting items in the rubble *after* the collapse were bad enough; and I have shown why I consider most, if not all, of those reports to be false. But ignoring trapped and injured victims *before* the collapse to sneak away with some new clothes would be evil on another level. Making such an accusation is gravely serious. If you're going to report it, you'd better have ironclad facts to back it up.

There are ironclad facts in this case. There are multiple eyewitness accounts, there's the physical evidence of the rig's location, there are survivors' (those rescued by Ladder 4) testimony, and there is video footage. But instead of backing up any allegation of wrongdoing, the facts tell the opposite. Unlike with so many others who died that day, we know what the members of Ladder 4 were doing up until the moment of their deaths. They were rescuing people. They knew the risks. They persisted in the face of horrific adversity. They exhibited the true spirit of the FDNY. Like so many other people in those buildings they rose to the occasion beautifully. They were not mythic heroes spitting in danger's eye. They were talented and imperfect; unsure yet determined; brave *and* scared; loving and loved. There was nothing at all mythic about their heroics—they were everyday heroes.

**

I spent years thinking William Langewiesche to be a scoundrel and a liar. I used to have this fantasy of seeing him in a restaurant and throwing a drink in his face— Hollywood style. *And maybe he would become indignant and we would fistfight and the newspaper headlines would say* 'American Ground *author beaten up by angry fireman.'* But from what I've read while researching this book—both written by and written about William Langewiesche—he does not strike me as someone who would intentionally fabricate a story. I think he believed the things he wrote, at least at the time. Spending time at the World Trade Center site produced strong emotions. My time at the site led to—among many things—my hatred of Langewiesche. His time at the site led to his resentment of firefighters. Our passions were shaped by our own experiences. I have presented my case for why his view was biased and I fully admit that my guttural reaction to his book was prejudicial in as much as I hated it before I had ever read it. But now I have.

Though Langewiesche would later claim he was only reporting what construction managers had told him about Ladder 4's excavation to highlight the construction side's negative feelings toward firemen,[159] that is not how he wrote it in *American Ground* (2002 version). He described the scene as if he were there. He may full well have believed the story and trusted what the superintendent told him, but he was not there. He got the story wrong.

I don't need him to be the villain—the vulture. My hate has dissipated. He can keep his resentment of firefighters. He did his time down at the site—he's entitled to his opinion. But he should admit that he got the Ladder 4 story wrong. Instead—both in interviews and later writings—he has doubled down on his claim that it was the public's misinterpretation of his book that is responsible for the controversy and not his hurtful repetition of a vicious lie.[160] He will probably never attempt to fix the pain that he caused the families of the men of Ladder 4. I'm through with waiting for him to do so. This is why I write.

CHAPTER 12

WERE YOU THERE ON 9/11? is a question I've been asked countless times. Tourists visiting the firehouse; people I meet while on vacation; strangers at dinner parties; my children's teachers: just about anyone who finds out I'm a firefighter wants to know what I did during what has become for this generation of Americans the equivalent of Pearl Harbor. I don't enjoy talking about 9/11 with people I hardly know. I feel like I'm justifying the fact that I wasn't killed. *No, I wasn't working that morning—but I was there. Yes, my firehouse was in Brooklyn—but five of our guys were killed.*

The only way to really do that day justice would be to recount every gory detail unfiltered. But how? How do I describe the sight of two skyscrapers smashed down over acres of downtown Manhattan? How do I tell them how it felt to look at a mountain of endless twisted steel and know that there were thousands of people underneath? How could I describe the look on Mike Ragusa's friend's face when I told him I didn't know where Mikey was? Should I tell them about the dead Port Authority cop I knelt beside for eight hours, coughing on smoke while that damned PASS alarm blared in my ears. Do I tell them how close John McLoughlin came to having the bottom parts of his legs gnawed off by a Sawzall? And what about Sally? Do I tell them how hard it was to tell Sally her son was dead? Or the funerals—do I talk about the hundreds of funerals? And Tipping. Do I tell them what exactly I found that gray and misty morning?

9/11 was not just a day. It was a year-long experience at the least. But I feel like trying to describe it as such to a stranger would make me seem to be either exaggerating, self-congratulating, or wallowing in self-pity. Still, I understand why people ask me about 9/11 and I don't blame them for their curiosity. It was for many people one of the most shocking and memorable events of their lifetime. Instead of some ghoulish quest for details, I take their curiosity for caring. The attacks on 9/11 were a deeply moving experience for Americans and they still feel the need to learn about it.

I usually give a sort of generic, non-committal answer. *Yes, I was there. Sure, it was a crazy day. Yes, many of my colleagues died.* I repeat back the information offered in the question and hope the conversation drifts toward a different topic. It is a contradictory reaction from someone who does not want people to stop talking about 9/11. I want people to remember. I want the history told. And most of all, I want the injustices that have been put forth so far, as history, corrected. But until now I have been reluctant to be the one to tell that history. Would talking about my experiences be self-serving? Would I be playing into Langewiesche's hand, seeking hero worship by association? I think the reason why I first wrote about Ladder 4's ordeal in a poem was to keep my story abstract—to remain one step removed from the verse's narrator.

Clearly, I did decide to write a history of 9/11. It is not an all-encompassing chronicle of the events but simply my own personal experience. How did I overcome my reluctance? First, I strived to avoid self-serving descriptions of events by presenting myself as little more than a witness. The closest thing in my first-hand account to heroics is probably my telling of John McLouglin's rescue. It was always my intent to stress the bravery of the rescuers who crawled under the beam and persevered to dig the sergeant out rather than portray any of my actions as particularly daring. In sum, I saw what those guys did and I wanted the world to know. Second, it was important for me to not become (in my writing) the self-righteous, thin-skinned, tribal boor put forth in *American Ground* as the prototypical fireman. I decided to treat William Langewiesche as fairly as possible.

Instead of starting with the premise that Langewiesche is a liar and cherry picking inaccuracies in his account to support my thesis, I put forth the instances in *American Ground* where he is critical of firefighters, acknowledged the rare instances of validity in his criticisms, and pointed out where the criticisms were based on misunderstandings. Mostly, however, I have attributed his censures to a bias rooted in his close ties to the chief engineers and construction managers who operated with aims often at odds with the Fire Department's mission at the site. All of this was done with the simple purpose of explaining to the reader where the allegations of looting made against Ladder 4 came from.

With no delusions of grandeur regarding my own contribution to the historical record of 9/11, what do I want the world to remember about the World Trade Center attacks? There is no need for me to reiterate the countless acts of selfless bravery performed on September 11, 2001 by civilians and first responders alike. Their tales are woven into the fabric of the tragedy's folklore. There have been a myriad of articles and books, films and television programs dedicated to these heroes. For all the controversy surrounding the 9/11 Museum at Ground Zero, the display does a beautiful job of telling the stories of many of the heroes who died that day—rightfully so. What I have tried to add to the narrative is the story of the daily struggle in the months following the attacks that members of the Fire Department endured. Of course, many others struggled during those times as well, but I am only qualified to speak about what the Fire Department went through. Most firefighters displayed an admirable level of dedication to duty during that difficult time and I feel that any critique of the FDNY's actions on 9/11 and during the rescue and recovery must include the many external stresses I've discussed as proper context for those actions.

If nothing else I've written about gets remembered, however, I'll settle for the world knowing that the men of Ladder 4 died rescuing people, not looting.

**

For those families who lost loved ones on 9/11 the tragedy has never really ended. Every day there are reminders of the precious lives that were stolen from them. For those who lost friends and colleagues, there is nothing to be done but carry on their memories. If the lost are alive in our hearts and in our minds than they *are* alive—maybe not in the way we want them to be, but it's all we have.

In the immediate aftermath of the World Trade Center collapse, my dad operated heavy machinery at the site and in the months after at the Staten Island Landfill during the recovery. My brother Joe watched the planes hit from his office window a few blocks away. He boarded a ferry to evacuate as the first tower collapsed. And Rob, my youngest brother who was one day out of the Fire Academy on 9/11, spent the night of September 11 operating a hose line and searching the site. He worked at the Trade Center site and at the landfill during the recovery. Reporting to his staging area may have saved his life on 9/11, but he couldn't escape the hidden danger. He was forced to retire from the Fire Department in 2012 after contracting numerous illnesses linked to his time spent at the World Trade Center rescue and recovery. He has undergone multiple operations and is often confined to bed. His wife struggles to take care of him and their three children—she knows as well as anyone that 9/11 is not over. Her father worked for Cantor Fitzgerald; he was killed that day. My nieces and nephew never met their grandfather. My family is like thousands of others in the New York area. September 11, 2001 has shaped our lives.

To date, the worst effects I've felt from 9/11 have not been physical, but something else. I've described many of the emotions I've struggled with in earlier chapters. Some emotions were harder to deal with than others and all have lessened with the passage of time. But somehow the anger I harbored over the accusations against Ladder 4 seemed to outlive most of the other emotional effects.

In researching this book, I interviewed a number of current and former members of Engine 54 and Ladder 4. They protested vehemently Langewiesche's claims when the book was released and rallied outside his book signing events to tell the world the truth. Interestingly, however, none of these members describe to me harboring the kind of lingering anger that I did. They are certain the allegations are false. They protested the book and then, for the most part, they moved on. That is not to imply that these guys are OK with Langewiesche in any way, only that none of them described to me having the level of obsession I did. Why?

Perhaps because they knew the deceased so well, their certainty of innocence overpowered anything some journalist could sling. Though I was no less certain of their innocence, because I did not know the men of Ladder 4 in life, I lacked the memories of their true nature to sustain a faith that eventually the world would see these men for who they really were. My passion for literature and history taught me well that not everything that gets recorded and passed down as fact is the truth. Time may have lessened my anger, and the love I've been lucky enough to be surrounded by—from my wife, and children, family and friends—may have led me to a certain peace. What I had yet to find, however, was the faith that justice would be done—that the truth would be told. Perhaps, like the members of Engine 54 and Ladder 4, I needed to look to the true nature of the men who died to find my faith.

**

John Tipping had moved away from his family to go to college in Charleston. Whether it was a streak of independence or a sense of adventure, John's need to strike out on his own was tempered by the calling to return and follow in his father's footsteps—a calling that came from within. It was his own decision to become a firefighter,[161] one that would transform him. "He matured as a person when he was in the Fire Department,"[162] Jack Tipping said of his son shortly after the attacks. John loved the job; he and his fellow firefighters became family.[163] The idea that John could have betrayed his oath—betrayed his family—is unthinkable.

"John was a young man who was not only full of life—but he also LIVED his life to the fullest," wrote a coworker from John's days in Charleston.[164] The common theme throughout his life is passion for living. From the soccer field, to the ski slopes, to the firehouse, he made the most out of his 33 years and deeply touched those around him. His parents guard his memory and his sisters tell his story. John's nieces and nephews will tell their children about what a wonderful man he was. To be loved is to live forever in the hearts of those who remain. *American*

Ground will exist in the future, but that does not mean it will live.

Like the loved ones of all the victims of 9/11, the families and friends of the men from Ladder 4 will ensure their memories—and their true spirits—live on. The depth of feelings expressed even now, so many years later, is hard to miss. It jumped out at me at every stage of my research for this book. In speaking with their coworkers and family and in writing, I found the connection I needed to give me faith that the truth can endure. I found anew the inspiration to live life to the fullest and never waste a minute to touch the lives of my loved ones. For the second time in my life, I found John Tipping.

Acknowledgments

SEPTEMBER 11, 2001 is a day that will be talked and written about for centuries to come. Many talented writers have already published comprehensive accounts of 9/11. I will leave the big picture to the professional historians and content myself with having simply jotted down my little piece of the puzzle. I have striven to present the most accurate account of events possible in what I would describe as part memoir, part investigative history. In the investigative passages, my first choice was always personal interviews with eyewitnesses and citations from primary sources of documentary evidence. When at times, these proved elusive, I relied on secondary sources from reputable outlets. In the memoir portions of the book, I have relied on my own memory of the events and wherever possible, corroborated my recollections with relevant witnesses.

It was important to me to include all the facts I discovered regardless of their convenience to my argument. Accordingly, witness statements are cited which could be interpreted as contradictory to other statements. I offer explanations for these contradictions, and included them precisely *because* they are contradictory. The facts speak for themselves and the evidence is overwhelming. I had no need to edit out inconvenient details. Many of the events I describe in the memoir sections took place 15-plus years prior to writing, but I worked very hard to present them not only to the best of my recollection, but fairly.

I am truly grateful to Charles Pellegrino for his scientific research into the collapse of the Twin Towers and Ladder 4's final moments. He was very kind in his letters to me and encouraged me in my research. I have no idea whether there is validity to the charges of dishonesty made toward him regarding his other book, but felt compelled to discuss the controversy (and its effect on my motivation to write) here in the spirit of full disclosure.

The writing of this book may have been a long road, but many people guided me along the way. Lenny Sieli and Billy Carlson pointed me in the right direction from the start. Ed Coyle, Joe Ceravolo, and Bob Jackson were all kind enough to give valuable background information on Engine 54 and Ladder 4's experience after 9/11. Jack Tipping was very gracious in taking the time to tell me about his son John. Paul Mallery and Patrick Drury were generous with their time in recounting the events they witnessed. Ed Morrison, Don Schneider, Chris Eysser, Fred Mallet, and Richie Murray all gave interviews this book would be much less colorful without. Tim Brown was a reservoir of knowledge on the city and nation's response to the 9/11 attacks. His interviews were invaluable and his story is captivating. Richie Portello, a mentor to me in the Fire Department, was always available for guidance and to bounce ideas off. And Sally Regenhard, whose strength through unbelievable tragedy always inspired me, once again showed me kindness in her reading of the manuscript. This book could not have been written without all of their help.

To the officers and firefighters of Engine 279 and Ladder 131, I will always feel a special bond with the brothers I went through 9/11 with. All of them stepped up selflessly after the attacks, but Kevin Dillion, Gary Kakeh, and Gerry Sweeney deserve special recognition.

I would also like to thank my editor, Susan Lunny Keag for her thorough reviews and perfect advice; as well as Kelly Kocinski Trager, whose professional expertise was indispensable to a reference-heavy nonfiction book.

And of course, my deepest gratitude goes to my wife, Teresa. From the time we met, she has lived with this story also. She has put up with me traveling all over the tri-state area tracking down interviews, and spending hours upon hours reading and researching, and watched me type draft after draft after draft. She supported me every step of the way, like she always does.

A.S.

BIBLIOGRAPHY

-- *American Vesuvius,* A & E Television Networks, 2006.

--Anderson, Jenny; Blake, Rich; Gold, Jacqueline S.; Gopinath, Deepak and Schack, Justin; edited and compiled by Ruth Hamel. "Where did everybody go?" *Institutional Investor Magazine,* October 1, 2001, www.institutionalinvestor.com/Article.aspx?ArticleID=10277 60&single=true#/.WPutojpCirc (4/22/17).

--Bahrampour, Tara *et al.* "A Nation Challenged: Portraits of Grief: The Victims; The Mystery of Computers, A Bicycle for Two, and the Tango Lesson," *New York Times,* February 24, 2002, www.nytimes.com/2002/02/24/nyregion/nation-challenged-portraits-grief-victims-mystery-computers-bicycle-for-two.html (3/3/18).

--Barry, Dan. "A Few Moments of Hope in a Mountain of Rubble," *New York Times,* September 13, 2001, events.nytimes.com/2001/09/13/nyregion/13RESC.html?pag ewanted=all (4/4/17).

--Boynton, Robert S. "William Langewiesche," *The New New Journalism: Conversations with America's Best Nonfiction Writers on Their Craft,* www.newnewjournalism.com/bio.php?last_name=langewiesc he (11/25/17).

--Cardwell, Diane. "City to Drop Charges Against 17 of 18 Firefighters Arrested Over Protest," *New York Times,* November 11, 2001, www.nytimes.com/2001/11/11/nyregion/city-to-drop-charges-against-17-of-18-firefighters-arrested-over-protest.html (3/2/18).

--Caron, Christina. "9/11 Firefighter Speaks with ABC News 10 Years Later," *ABC News,* September 7, 2011, abcnews.go.com/US/September_11/911-firefighter-speaks-abc-news-10-years/story?id=14456184 (2/26/18).

--Carr, David. "Rebutting a Claim of Tarnished Valor; Research Challenges Account of 9/11 Looting by Firefighters," *New York Times,* March 23, 2003, www.nytimes.com/2003/03/23/nyregion/rebutting-claim-tarnished-valor-research-challenges-account-9-11-looting.html (4/28/2017).

--Cauchon, Dennis and Moore, Martha T. "Plunge Just the Start of Nightmare," *USA Today,* September 4, 2002, usatoday.com/news/sept11/2002-09-04-elevator-young-usat_x.htm (4/1/18).

--Cauchon, Dennis and Moore, Martha T. "Elevators Were Disaster Within Disaster," *USA Today,* September 4, 2002, usatoday30.usatoday.com/news/sept11/2002-09-04-elevator-usat_x.htm (3/23/18).

--Conan, Neal (Radio Broadcast Interview). "Talk of the Nation," November 20, 2002, *NPR,* transcript provided by *NPR* Audience Relations.

--Dwyer, Jim and Flynn, Kevin. *102 Minutes: The Unforgettable Story of the Fight to Survive Inside the Twin Towers* (New York: Times Books, 2005).

--Falco, Nicole. "He 'Answered... the Call of God,'" *LIHerald.com,* October 18, 2001, liherald.com/stories/He-answeredthe-call-to-God,17986 (3/3/18).

--Fire Department City of New York Manhattan dispatcher frequency recordings for September 11, 2001, archived online at archive.org/details/911_fdny_dispatches.

--Gibbs, Kimberly. "Untitled," *John J. Tipping Condolences,* May 5, 2015, www.legacy.com/guestbooks/john-j-tipping-condolences/124939?page=6 (11/27/17).

--Goldberg, Jeffrey. "Reverse Engineering," review of *American Ground: Unbuilding the World Trade Center,* by William Langewiesche. *New York Times,* October 20, 2002, www.nytimes.com/2002/10/20/books/reverse-engineering.html (6/7/17).

--Italiano, Laura. "Ransacking Rats Ignored Death All Around Them," *New York Post,* November 25, 2001, nypost.com/2001/11/25/ransacking-rats-ignored-death-all-around-them/ (11/27/17).

--Langewiesche, William. *American Ground: Unbuilding the World Trade Center* (New York: North Point Press, 2002).

--Lipton, Eric and Glanz, James. "A Nation Challenged: Ground Zero; Remains of 11 Firefighters Are Found at Trade Center," *New York Times,* March 13, 2002, www.nytimes.com/2002/03/13/nyregion/nation-challenged-ground-zero-remains-11-firefighters-are-found-trade-center.html (3/12/17).

--Liss, Rebecca. "Oliver Stone's World Trade Center Fiction: How the Rescue Really Happened," *Slate,* August 9, 2006, www.slate.com/articles/news_and_politics/life_and_art/2006/08/oliver_stones_world_trade_center_fiction.html (11/26/17).

--Moore, Elizabeth. "Joseph Angelini Jr. A Firefighter Passionate About Gardening," *Newsday,* October 22, 2001, posted online at blog.nj.com/njv_fausta_wertz/2008/09/september_11_i_remember_joseph.html (3/14/18).

--National Fallen Firefighters Foundation, "Roll of Honor: Michael H. Haub,"   www.firehero.org/fallen-firefighter/michael-h-haub/ (3/3/18).

--O'Neill, Helen. "One Year Later, We're Still Burying Our Dead," *Boston Globe,* 2002, archive.boston.com/news/packages/sept11/anniversary/wir e_stories/0911_firehouse_revisited.htm (3/21/17).

--Pellegrino, Charles. *Ghosts of Vesuvius: A New Look at the Last Days of Pompeii, How the Towers Fell, and Other Strange Connections* (New York: Harper Perennial, 2004).

--Pentchoukov, Ivan. "Firehouse That Lost 15 on 9/11 Hosts Mets," *The Epoch Times,* September 11, 2013, www.theepochtimes.com/firehouse-that-lost-15-on-911-hosts-mets_284003.html (3/10/18).

--Peterson, Helen. "Charges vs. Firefighters Dropped," *New York Daily News,* December 19, 2001, www.nydailynews.com/archives/news/charges-firefighters-dropped-article-1.917066 (3/2/18).

--Port Authority Audio Repeater recordings for September 11, 2001, archived online at archive.org/details/911_fdny_dispatches.

--*Portraits: 9/11/01: The Collected 'Portraits of Grief' from the New York Times* (New York: Times Books-Henry Holt & Co., 2002).

--*Publishers Weekly* review dated September 16, 2002, www.publishersweekly.com/978-0-86547-582-3 (11/25/17).

--Raynovich, William. "Crushed: How Proper Treatment of Crush Syndrome Saved Police Sgt. John McLoughlin after 22 Hours under WTC Rubble," *Journal of Emergency Medical Services,* August 31, 2006, www.jems.com/articles/print/volume-31/issue-9/features/crushed.html (4/4/17).

--Rich, Motoko. "Pondering Good Faith in Publishing," *New York Times,* March 8, 2010, www.nytimes.com/2010/03/09/books/09publishers.html (11/26/17).

--Robinson, Ed. "'Liar!' Firestorm; FDNY Rally Hits Writer's Loot Claim," *New York Post,* November 19, 2002, nypost.com/2002/11/19/liar-firestorm-fdny-rally-hits-writers-loot-claim/ (2/27/18).

--Rose, Derek. "Fireman Mourned at Wake," *New York Daily News,* March 21, 2002, www.nydailynews.com/archives/news/fireman-mourned-wake-article-1.480547 (3/3/18).

--"Samuel P. Oitice Obituary," *The Journal News,* October 30, 2001 reprinted at www.legacy.com/obituaries/lohud/obituary.aspx?page=lifestory&pid=148867110 (11/25/17).

--Slepian, Stephanie. "Anthony Rodriguez, 36, Firefighter for Just 6 Months," *Staten Island Advance,* October 22, 2001, (updated 8/5/11) www.silive.com/september-11/index.ssf/2010/09/anthony_rodriguez_36_firefight.html (3/16/18).

--Smith, Dennis. *Report from Ground Zero* (New York: Viking, 2002).

--Steinhauer, Jennifer. "A Nation Challenged: Ground Zero; Ex-Firefighter's Quiet Plea Ends Conflict Over Staffing," Novenmber 17, 2001, www.nytimes.com/2001/11/17/nyregion/nation-challenged-ground-zero-ex-firefighter-s-quiet-plea-ends-conflict-over.html (3/2/18).

--Wellin, Kathryn. "John James Tipping II: He Enjoyed Many Rugged Sports," *Newsday,* October 14, 2001 posted online at bravestmemorial.net/html/members_individual/tipping_john /newsday_com.html (3/12/18).

--World Trade Center 911 FDNY Telephone Calls September 11, 2001 Audio, *City of New York,* 2006.

--Worth, Robert (compiled by Anthony Ramirez). "Firefighter Impersonator Pleads," *New York Times,* February 22, 2002, www.nytimes.com/2002/02/22/nyregion/metro-briefing-new-york-manhattan-firefighter-impersonator-pleads.html (11/27/17).

NOTES

*The version of *American Ground: Unbuilding the World Trade Center,* by William Langewiesche cited in this book is the 2002 hardcover edition by North Point Press. Exceptions, where the 2011 paperback edition by Simon & Schuster is cited, are noted either in the text or the notes.

---

1 *Portraits: 9/11/01: The Collected 'Portraits of Grief' from the New York Times* (New York: Times Books-Henry Holt & Co., 2002), 367.
2 Rhonda O'Callaghan quoted in *Portraits: 9/11/01,* 367.
3 *Ibid.*
4 *Portraits: 9/11/01,* 16.
5 Donna Angelini quoted in Elizabeth Moore, "Joseph Angelini Jr. A Firefighter Passionate About Gardening," *Newsday,* October 22, 2001, posted online at blog.nj.com/njv_fausta_wertz/2008/09/september_11_i_reme mber_joseph.html (3/14/18).
6 *Ibid.*
7 Tara Bahrampour *et al.,* "A Nation Challenged: Portraits of Grief: The Victims; The Mystery of Computers, A Bicycle for Two, and the Tango Lesson," *New York Times,* February 24, 2002, www.nytimes.com/2002/02/24/nyregion/nation-challenged-portraits-grief-victims-mystery-computers-bicycle-for-two.html (3/3/18).
8 Tim Brown interview with author, October 27, 2017.
9 Tim Brown interview with author, October 27, 2017.
10 Nicole Falco, "He 'Answered... the Call of God,'" *LIHerald.com,* October 18, 2001, liherald.com/stories/He-answeredthe-call-to-God,17986 (3/3/18).
11 National Fallen Firefighters Foundation, "Roll of Honor: Michael H. Haub," www.firehero.org/fallen-firefighter/michael-h-haub/ (3/3/18).
12 Derek Rose, "Fireman Mourned at Wake," *New York Daily News,* March 21, 2002, www.nydailynews.com/archives/news/fireman-mourned-wake-article-1.480547 (3/3/18).

[13]"Samuel P. Oitice Obituary," *The Journal News,* October 30, 2001 reprinted at www.legacy.com/obituaries/lohud/obituary.aspx?page=lifest ory&pid=148867110 (11/25/17).

[14] Tim Brown interview with author, October 27, 2017.

[15] *Portraits: 9/11/01,* 55-56.

[16] *Ibid.*

[17] Kathryn Wellin "John James Tipping II: He Enjoyed Many Rugged Sports," *Newsday,* October 14, 2001 posted online at bravestmemorial.net/html/members_individual/tipping_john /newsday_com.html (3/12/18).

[18] *Ibid.*

[19] Robert S. Boynton, "William Langewiesche," *The New New Journalism: Conversations with America's Best Nonfiction Writers on Their Craft,* www.newnewjournalism.com/bio.php?last_name=langewiesc he (11/25/17).

[20] *Ibid.*

[21] *Ibid.*

[22] *Ibid.*

[23] William Langewiesche, *American Ground: Unbuilding the World Trade Center* (New York: North Point Press, 2002), 160.

[24] Langewiesche, 161.

[25] Ed Robinson, "'Liar!' Firestorm; FDNY Rally Hits Writer's Loot Claim," *New York Post,* November 19, 2002, nypost.com/2002/11/19/liar-firestorm-fdny-rally-hits-writers-loot-claim/ (2/27/18).

[26] Jeffrey Goldberg, "Reverse Engineering," review of *American Ground: Unbuilding the World Trade Center,* by William Langewiesche. *New York Times,* October 20, 2002, www.nytimes.com/2002/10/20/books/reverse-engineering.html (6/7/17).

[27] Goldberg.

[28] *Publishers Weekly* review dated September 16, 2002, www.publishersweekly.com/978-0-86547-582-3 (11/25/17).

[29] Ed Morrison phone interview with author, January 23, 2018.

[30] Ed Morrison phone interview with author, January 23, 2018.

[31] Don Schneider phone interview with author, April 12, 2017.

[32] Don Schneider phone interview with author, April 12, 2017.

[33] William Raynovich, "Crushed: How Proper Treatment of Crush Syndrome Saved Police Sgt. John McLoughlin after 22 Hours under WTC Rubble," *Journal of Emergency Medical Services,* August 31, 2006, www.jems.com/articles/print/volume-31/issue-9/features/crushed.html (4/4/17).

[34] Rebecca Liss, "Oliver Stone's World Trade Center Fiction: How the Rescue Really Happened," *Slate,* August 9, 2006, www.slate.com/articles/news_and_politics/life_and_art/2006/08/oliver_stones_world_trade_center_fiction.html (11/26/17).

[35] Chris Eysser phone interview with author, March 28, 2017.

[36] Chris Eysser phone interview with author, March 28, 2017.

[37] Fred Mallett phone interview with author, July 12, 2017.

[38] Fred Mallett phone interview with author, March 7, 2018.

[39] Stephanie Slepian, "Anthony Rodriguez, 36, Firefighter for Just 6 Months," *Staten Island Advance,* October 22, 2001, (updated 8/5/11) www.silive.com/september-11/index.ssf/2010/09/anthony_rodriguez_36_firefight.html (3/16/18).

[40] *Ibid.*

[41] Richie Murray phone interview with author, March 6, 2018.

[42] Richie Murray phone interview with author, March 6, 2018.

[43] Richie Murray phone interview with author, March 6, 2018.

[44] Richie Murray phone interview with author, March 6, 2018.

[45] Richie Murray phone interview with author, March 6, 2018.

[46] Richie Murray phone interview with author, March 6, 2018.

[47] Richie Murray phone interview with author, March 6, 2018.

[48] Helen O'Neill, "One Year Later, We're Still Burying Our Dead," *Boston Globe,* 2002, archive.boston.com/news/packages/sept11/anniversary/wire_stories/0911_firehouse_revisited.htm (3/21/17).

[49] Bob Jackson quoted in O'Neill.

[50] Joe Ceravolo quoted in Ivan Pentchoukov, "Firehouse That Lost 15 on 9/11 Hosts Mets," *The Epoch Times,* September 11,

2013,   www.theepochtimes.com/firehouse-that-lost-15-on-911-hosts-mets_284003.html (3/10/18).

[51] *Ibid.*

[52] Joseph Nardone audio clip played during Interview with Neal Conan, "Talk of the Nation," November 20, 2002, *NPR,* transcript provided by *NPR* Audience Relations.

[53] *American Vesuvius,* A & E Television Networks, 2006.

[54] Charles Pellegrino, *Ghosts of Vesuvius: A New Look at the Last Days of Pompeii, How the Towers Fell, and Other Strange Connections* (New York: Harper Perennial, 2004).

[55] Pellegrino, 408.

[56] *Ibid.*

[57] *Ibid.*

[58] Pellegrino, 408-409.

[59] Pellegrino, 410.

[60] Pellegrino, 410-412.

[61] Pellegrino, 411-413.

[62] Pellegrino, 414-415.

[63] Motoko Rich, "Pondering Good Faith in Publishing," *New York Times,* March 8, 2010, www.nytimes.com/2010/03/09/books/09publishers.html (11/26/17).

[64] *Ibid.*

[65] Fire Department City of New York Manhattan dispatcher frequency recordings for September 11, 2001, archived online at archive.org/details/911_fdny_dispatches.

[66] World Trade Center 911 FDNY Telephone Calls September 11, 2001 Audio, *City of New York,* 2006.

[67] Fire Department City of New York Manhattan dispatcher frequency recordings for September 11, 2001, archived online at archive.org/details/911_fdny_dispatches.

[68] Paul Mallery interview with author, April 25, 2017 and Tim Brown interview with author, April 21, 2017.

[69] Tim Brown interview with author, April 21, 2017.

[70] Tim Brown interview with author, April 21, 2017.

[71] Tim Brown interview with author, April 21, 2017.

[72] Tim Brown interview with author, April 21, 2017.

[73] Tim Brown interview with author, April 21, 2017.

[74] Tim Brown interview with author, April 21, 2017.

[75] Jim Dwyer and Kevin Flynn, *102 Minutes: The Unforgettable Story of the Fight to Survive Inside the Twin Towers* (New York: Times Books, 2005), 157.

[76] Dennis Cauchon, Martha T. Moore, "Plunge Just the Start of Nightmare," *USA Today,* September 4, 2002, usatoday.com/news/sept11/2002-09-04-elevator-young-usat_x.htm (4/1/18).

[77] *Ibid.*

[78] Dwyer and Flynn, 157-158.

[79] Ladder 4's time of arrival estimated based on research of George Black (see note 104 below) and transmission time of Lieutenant Daniel O'Callaghan of Ladder 4 confirming Ladder 4's assignment (see note 65).

[80] Lauren Smith quoted in Jenny Anderson, Rich Blake, Jacqueline S. Gold, Deepak Gopinath and Justin Schack; edited and compiled by Ruth Hamel, "Where did everybody go?" *Institutional Investor Magazine,* October 1, 2001, www.institutionalinvestor.com/Article.aspx?ArticleID=10277 60&single=true#/.WPutojpCirc (4/22/17).

[81] *Ibid.*

[82] Dwyer and Flynn, 158.

[83] Dwyer and Flynn, 157-159.

[84] Lauren Smith quoted in Anderson *et al.*

[85] Based on Tim Brown's and Paul Mallery's accounts and the fact that Ladder 4's Hurst Tool was later found in the debris in this area.

[86] Anderson *et al.*

[87] O'Neill.

[88] Tim Brown interview with author, April 21, 2017 and Dennis Cauchon and Martha T. Moore, "Elevators Were Disaster Within Disaster," *USA Today,* September 4, 2002, usatoday30.usatoday.com/news/sept11/2002-09-04-elevator-usat_x.htm (3/23/18).

[89] Eric Lipton and James Glanz, "A Nation Challenged: Ground Zero; Remains of 11 Firefighters Are Found at Trade Center,"

New York Times, March 13, 2002, www.nytimes.com/2002/03/13/nyregion/nation-challenged-ground-zero-remains-11-firefighters-are-found-trade-center.html (3/12/17) and Cauchon and Moore, "Elevators Were Disaster Within Disaster."

[90] Tim Brown interview with author, April 21, 2017.

[91] Paul Mallery interview with author, April 25, 2017.

[92] Paul Mallery interview with author, April 25, 2017.

[93] Paul Mallery interview with author, April 25, 2017.

[94] Paul Mallery interview with author, April 25, 2017.

[95] Tim Brown interview with author, April 21, 2017.

[96] Paul Mallery interview with author, April 25, 2017.

[97] Langewiesche, 161.

[98] Langewiesche, 160.

[99] Interview with Neal Conan, "Talk of the Nation," November 20, 2002, *NPR,* transcript provided by *NPR* Audience Relations.

[100] *Ibid.*

[101] *Ibid.*

[102] *Ibid.*

[103] Langewiesche, 161.

[104] George Black's research and subsequent campaign to clear Ladder 4's name was chronicled by David Carr in a 2003 *New York Times* article (David Carr, "Rebutting a Claim of Tarnished Valor; Research Challenges Account of 9/11 Looting by Firefighters," *New York Times,* March 23, 2003, accessed online 4/28/2017). The Carr article is the source of information on Black's research.

[105] Patrick Drury phone interview with author, April 8, 2017.

[106] Reprinted with Patrick Drury's permission.

[107] Langewiesche, 161.

[108] Don Schneider phone interviews with author, April 12, 2017 and March 6, 2018.

[109] Don Schneider phone interviews with author, April 12, 2017 and March 6, 2018.

[110] Don Schneider phone interview with author, March 6, 2018.

[111] Don Schneider phone interview with author, March 6, 2018.

[112] Langewiesche, 67, 69, 132, 146, 156.

113 Langewiesche, 69.

114 *Ibid.*

115 Langewiesche, 16.

116 *Ibid.*

117 Langewiesche, 159.

118 *Ibid.*

119 Robert Worth (compiled by Anthony Ramirez), "Firefighter Impersonator Pleads," *New York Times,* February 22, 2002, www.nytimes.com/2002/02/22/nyregion/metro-briefing-new-york-manhattan-firefighter-impersonator-pleads.html (11/27/17).

120 Laura Italiano, "Ransacking Rats Ignored Death All Around Them," *New York Post,* November 25, 2001, nypost.com/2001/11/25/ransacking-rats-ignored-death-all-around-them/ (11/27/17).

121 Interview with Neal Conan, "Talk of the Nation," November 20, 2002, *NPR,* transcript provided by *NPR* Audience Relations.

122 Langewiesche, 160.

123 Thomas E. Franklin's famous picture of three firefighters raising the American flag on 9/11 is posted at thomasefranklin.com (as of 3/20/18).

124 Christina Caron, "9/11 Firefighter Speaks with ABC News 10 Years Later," *ABC News,* September 7, 2011, abcnews.go.com/US/September_11/911-firefighter-speaks-abc-news-10-years/story?id=14456184 (2/26/18).

125 Langewiesche, 156.

126 *Ibid.*

127 *Ibid.*

128 See Port Authority Audio Repeater recordings, as well as eyewitness accounts of Tim Brown, Paul Mallery, and also Lauren Smith, as well as the many other published accounts of 9/11 recounting firefighters' actions before the collapse.

129 Port Authority Audio Repeater recordings for September 11, 2001, archived online at archive.org/details/911_fdny_dispatches.

130 1:07:54 Port Authority Audio Repeater.

131 1:11:48 Port Authority Audio Repeater.

[132] 1:10:48 Port Authority Audio Repeater.
[133] This video clip was posted at www.youtube.com/watch?v=a2nCQTEwGgA, as of 3/12/18.
[134] Tim Brown interview with author, April 21, 2017.
[135] Langewiesche, 158.
[136] *Ibid.*
[137] Langewiesche, 135.
[138] Langewiesche, 184.
[139] Langewiesche, 181.
[140] Langewiesche, 9.
[141] Langewiesche, 145-154.
[142] Dennis Smith, *Report from Ground Zero* (New York: Viking, 2002), 339-343.
[143] Smith, 339-343.
[144] This firefighter requested to remain anonymous. Phone interview with author, April 12, 2017.
[145] Smith, 342.
[146] *Ibid.*
[147] *Ibid.*
[148] Langewiesche, 151.
[149] *Ibid.*
[150] Diane Cardwell, "City to Drop Charges Against 17 of 18 Firefighters Arrested Over Protest," *New York Times,* November 11, 2001, www.nytimes.com/2001/11/11/nyregion/city-to-drop-charges-against-17-of-18-firefighters-arrested-over-protest.html (3/2/18); and Helen Peterson, "Charges vs. Firefighters Dropped," *New York Daily News,* December 19, 2001, www.nydailynews.com/archives/news/charges-firefighters-dropped-article-1.917066 (3/2/18).
[151] Jennifer Steinhauer, "A Nation Challenged: Ground Zero; Ex-Firefighter's Quiet Plea Ends Conflict Over Staffing," Novenmber 17, 2001, www.nytimes.com/2001/11/17/nyregion/nation-challenged-ground-zero-ex-firefighter-s-quiet-plea-ends-conflict-over.html (3/2/18).
[152] Langewiesche, 22-23, 96-99, 147, 160, 179, 202-203.

[153] Examples of Langewiesche's portrayal of firefighters as 'irrational, self-centered, boorish... basking in public's adoration and buying into their own inflated sense of loss' include passages on pp. 145, 150, 152, 157-158, 164 and throughout *American Ground.*

[154] Langewiesche, 160, 163-164.

[155] Langewiesche, 134.

[156] Dan Barry, "A Few Moments of Hope in a Mountain of Rubble," *New York Times,* September 13, 2001, events.nytimes.com/2001/09/13/nyregion/13RESC.html?pagewanted=all (4/4/17).

[157] Langewiesche, 160, 163-164.

[158] Langewiesche, 160.

[159] Interview with Neal Conan, "Talk of the Nation," November 20, 2002, *NPR,* transcript provided by *NPR* Audience Relations.

[160] See *NPR* interview with Neal Conan and the afterword to the 2011 paperback edition of *American Ground* (Simon & Schuster) 217-218.

[161] Jack Tipping phone interview with author, August 10, 2017.

[162] Jack Tipping quoted in *Portraits: 9/11/01,* 500.

[163] Jack Tipping phone interview with author, August 10, 2017.

[164] Kimberly Gibbs, "Untitled," *John J. Tipping Condolences,* May 5, 2015, www.legacy.com/guestbooks/john-j-tipping-condolences/124939?page=6 (11/27/17).